Popcorn for Breakfast

Poetry for people
who would not normally
read poetry.

Gerry Furney

Order this book online at www.trafford.com
or email orders@trafford.com

Most Trafford titles are also available at major online book retailers.

Printed in Victoria, BC, Canada.

ISBN: 978-1-4269-2436-1

Library of Congress Control Number: 2010900984

*Our mission is to efficiently provide the world's finest, most comprehensive book publishing
service, enabling every author to experience success. To find out how to publish your book, your
way, and have it available worldwide, visit us online at www.trafford.com*

Trafford rev. 05/05/2010

 www.trafford.com

North America & international
toll-free: 1 888 232 4444 (USA & Canada)
phone: 250 383 6864 ♦ fax: 812 355 4082

ACKNOWLEDGEMENTS

Very special thanks to Margaret Page and Sue Harvey whose technical knowledge and patience helped to create this book.

My wife, Carmel, handled the proof-reading challenges and her advice was invaluable. Her love of the English language kept me generally on the straight and narrow.

I am very grateful to Heather Brown for her black and white illustrations of loggers at work. She is a talented artist in many mediums.

Nick Yunge-Bateman provided the old photo of Telegraph Cove.

Stu Crabe took the aerial photo of the Town of Port McNeill from a helicopter provided by West Coast Helicopters.

Robin Quirk took the "one in a million" photo of the five killer whales.

TO MY WIFE CARMEL.

PREFACE

One of the more prominent members of our community is our long time mayor Gerry Furney. While Gerry's roots are in Ireland, he can speak of the old days of Port McNeill, old days that go back to when our town was a logging camp. He and his wife Carmel, with their daughter Liza and their son James seem to have a special spot in their hearts for this community. They've all made it their home and are involved in various visible ways in the community.

There are many things the citizens of our town admire about Gerry. Not only is he a thinking man, and a persuasive one at that, but he's also endowed with a good measure of common sense, and has never lost his common touch. There are few people in town he does not recognize, and it is doubtful that there are any who don't recognize him. He can be seen at the local arena cheering on his grandchildren or admiring them at school concerts. He is officially recognized at ice carnivals, school graduation ceremonies, and many other local events. Respect for Gerry goes well beyond this town of close to three thousand. Among government and business people in the province he is highly regarded.

With this background in mind, who would suspect that Gerry is also a poet, and a good one! His style of poetry has been influenced by some of the leading eighteenth century writers most notable the Anglo-Irish dramatist, writer and poet Oliver Goldsmith. Gerry's poems extol the common man and many things we enjoy, but take for granted. His poems give us the flavor of Gerry's humor.

To me it would be a shame if many people could not enjoy Gerry's poetry, his humor and his observations of man's follies, so I am pleased to offer these introductory notes to his most enjoyable and uniquely titled book of poems, **Popcorn for Breakfast.**

Werner Manke

Author of **Secrets of Hawking Manor**

INTRODUCTION

This is a book of poems that has been inspired by my experiences growing up in Cork, Ireland, spending two great years in London, England and emigrating to Port McNeill, British Columbia, where I have lived since 1956.

Writing these poems has been a most enjoyable experience for me. They are fairly basic in their composition and I do not offer them as poetry in the classical sense.

I have read many poems by "real" poets such as Oliver Goldsmith, Robert Service, Rudyard Kipling, Robert Swanson and Peter Trower. These "real" poets provided the inspiration for me to get more serious about my own efforts.

For poems whose content is self-explanatory, I have not given any explanation here.

For poems that might otherwise raise questions in a reader's mind, I have tried to provide enough details on each so that you will understand why they were written.

I hope that you will find at least a few poems here, that you will enjoy.

You, after all, are the reason that my poems have been assembled and published.

If you are happy with the selection and variety, that would be wonderful. Otherwise, read the last poem in the book, it's dedicated to you with my best wishes.

Gerry Furney

Contents

BROWSER, PLEASE YOURSELF

You're wondering what this book is all about

And if you should take time to check it out.

So to be fair and save you wasting time,

You should be conscious of the fact that I'm

The kind of guy who really likes to write,

On simple things in which I take delight.

I sometimes like to take a little poke

At silly, thoughtless, egoistic folk.

And sometimes when I have a worthy thought,

I write a little poem, just as I ought.

Among these poems you'll see I've broken rules,

They're simple but contain some little jewels.

And should you have a yen to criticize,

There is a simple point to realize.

You may not like the subjects or the rhymes,

But they recount some interesting times.

Most of the people who will own this book,

Would normally not give a poem a look.

But I am hoping that I'll catch your eye

And you will feel the urge that you should buy.

So here's a chance to really please yourself,

Just do not leave this book upon the shelf.

It's really up to you, my browsing friend,

So buy this book, enjoy it to the end.

POPCORN FOR BREAKFAST

Hockey for my kids was more than a sport,

We'd not miss a game or leave the team short.

Ice hockey practices, most of the games,

Were early each morn for Liza and James.

Bob Tyson our Coach, Assistant Bing T,

Were always on hand to ensure that we,

The parents of each of these little tykes

Looked after their needs, their wants and their likes.

But, as a rule rink Concessions were closed,

All rinks are the same, why, nobody knows.

You'd think they'd be keen to generate cash,

Being closed for business seems ever so rash.

So we relied on Concession machines,

For food and drink for these hockey teams.

And of the junk food that I ate there first

Popcorn for breakfast was surely the worst.

The coffee was stale, the hot chocolate cold,

Sandwiches tasteless except for the mould.

We'd check the machines to see what they had,

To say the least, the selection was bad.

There was one machine that never broke down,

With enough popcorn to feed a small town.

Continue.........

Continued………

Young hockey players need strength in their legs,

Should have a breakfast of bacon and eggs.

Our closest rink was a thirty-mile drive,

Be on the ice at five fifty-five.

So, out of the house by twenty past four,

We then drove around to pick up three more.

In just a minute they're all fast asleep,

While Dad drives with care through snow often deep,

Fully aware of the care he must take,

To stay on the road, not slide in the lake.

The drive takes an hour through forest so dark,

Five cars at the ice rink, no problem to park,

As close as we can beside the front door,

Just as five kids are beginning to snore.

I shake them awake from out of their dreams,

That's what it's like for these early morn teams.

They each grab a bag, while I take the sticks,

I check my watch, it is twenty to six.

Into the dressing room, rush to get dressed,

Onto the ice, just a little bit stressed.

I sit in the bleachers, watching them play,

Eating cold **POPCORN FOR BREAKFAST** each day.

Having two kids in hockey meant a lot of early morning drives to ice arenas in other towns. Teams need competition and we played in virtually every arena on Vancouver Island. There is one thing in common about arenas. They rarely have an open concession stand for early morning games as there are so few customers around. There are, however, machines that sell drinks, candy bars and popcorn, lots of popcorn! Hence, my poem on my least favourite breakfast, popcorn.

A CLUB OF ONE

Success for many people in this life,

Means that their social calendar is rife

With invitations to go here and there,

It keeps them busy with no time to spare.

Their lives are spent at meetings of their clubs,

At halls and homes and sometimes even pubs.

Committees take up so much of their time

As through the Chairs and Offices they climb.

The thought of such involvement scares me stiff,

I could become a busy member, if,

I drop my guard and say, "Yes", when they call,

They have the lowest standards after all.

A club that would accept me on their team

Must hold themselves in very low esteem.

In fact, I think it would be a disgrace,

If on their members' list, my name they'd place.

I know I'll miss the friendship, laughs and fun,

But I will just remain a club of one.

A famous Irish playwright, Brendan Behan, (1923-1964), refused an invitation to join a well-known club in London, on the excuse that its standards were too low, if they would accept him as a member. This poem is dedicated to him.

A HEALTHY APPETITE

You do not have to be so bright,

To understand man's appetite

For beauty in the other sex,

With woman Queen and man as Rex.

And just like all the Kings of old,

Your average man will be so bold

To let his 'magination roam

When he is far away from home,

To think what it just might be like

If he could overcome the psyche

That makes him understand the rule,

With other women do not fool.

And if his wife has any sense,

She'll patiently not take offense.

A clever woman will delight

In husband's healthy appetite.

From whence it comes she does not care,

A healthy appetite is rare.

So he may travel, he may roam,

But he must always eat at home.

The message in this poem is in the last few lines.

A HEARTY AND HEART-WARMING BREAKFAST

A lazy Sunday morning in Vancouver.

Let's not eat at the hotel, too fancy,

Drive around looking for a quirky breakfast kind of place.

Pass all the fancy places on Broadway,

Hit the corner of Main and Broadway.

A corner that never sleeps.

Take a right on Main

Spot a "hole in the wall" café. "Ping's"

Looks busy, must be popular, park, push door open

Loud voice of the lone waitress

"Wanna menu, coffee?"

Take the only empty booth

Hot coffee splashed in our cups

Instantly, simultaneously.

Look around, read the menus,

A motley crew of Saturday night flotsam,

Chattering, supping and chomping happily.

We order the "Full Canadian"

From the waitress, owner, manager,

Who virtually runs to a hatch

At the back of the café

And shouts to her husband, the Chef, cook, dishwasher.

In a mixture of broken English and Chinese.

Minutes later, two large plates,

Freshly cooked bacon, sausages, eggs and golden fried potatoes,

Were placed in front of us.

Continued………

Continued.........

Time to savour the breakfast, the atmosphere.

And the bottomless coffee cups.

Waitress keeping two dozen customers happy.

A blind man stumbles through the door.

Led by his guide dog.

Sits at the vacant single table beside our booth.

Fastest waitress on earth

Puts a mug of coffee in front of him

"Your usual, eh, be right there"

Another shout through the hatch

And a "Full Canadian"

Is placed gently in front of him.

She picks up the blind man's knife and fork,

Cuts his breakfast into bite-size pieces

And puts the knife and fork in his hands.

"I get you more coffee" she says,

Embarrassed by his heartfelt thank-you's.

Now there is a restaurant

That should be written up

In the Gourmet Guide.

A LUCKY CORK BOY'S SUMMER HOLIDAY

Saving a few pennies, some weeks,
Sometimes a few shillings,
By June my mother would announce,
"We have enough saved
To pay for a holiday at the seaside."
Start planning the things to bring.....
The anticipation was a holiday in itself.
Pack the bags with the essentials,
Especially the toys.
We'd take our sandals,
But never wore them,
Except going to Mass.
Youghal was like that,
A barefooted holiday place.
A steam-train ride for thirty miles.
Only thirty miles,
But a whole world away from the City of Cork.
Excitement mounting as the train passed Killeagh,
Arrival in Youghal to the sound of venting steam,
Watching the Guard pass a brass baton
To the Station Master, in his blue uniform,
A safety precaution. The track was clear.
Making our way through the crowd
That always assembled to meet the train.
Towards our lodging in the Back Strand.
A hurried hallo to our landlady,
Mrs. Fitzgerald of "St. Teresa's",
Dropping our bags and our shoes
In our tiny two-bed room,
Which Mrs Fitzgerald called a suite,
And running off barefooted
With our togs and our towels
To the Strand and its salty sea-weedy smell.
And a rush to the cold frothy waves,
To see who'd get wet first.
Our Summer holiday had begun.......

(Author, 3rd from left back row)

A MUSICAL NOTE

There's not a greater pleasure in this land,

Than sitting in with others in a band.

The type of music is of little note,

To tackle different types we're nothing loathe.

We'll try out marches, waltzes and dance tunes.

We've even got a guy who plays the spoons.

The brassy sounds are played by three trombones,

While saxophones provide the sweeter tones.

Our clarinets can play both high and low,

With dulcet notes from violin and bow.

Our trumpets sound the high notes of the brass,

The French horn adds a sparkling touch of class.

The piccolo and flutes are always there,

Their contributions sounding sweet and clear.

Our rhythm group, piano, bass and drums,

Provide a beat as lively as it comes.

Last year we entered in the Nationals' Test,

A Silver Medal placed us with the best.

There's just no easy way to even measure,

Just how this group provides me with such pleasure.

Dedicated to the members of the North Island Concert Band, winners of the Silver Medal at the Canadian National Band Competition held in Richmond (Vancouver), B.C. in 2006.

(Author, 3rd from left back row)

ANON

My dearest Walter and Eileen,

It's been some time since we have seen

The two of you with all your friends,

Partaking in poetic trends.

A deep discussion we have had,

On changing weather good and bad.

Inclement weather blowing snow,

Just makes it quite unsafe to go.

And, that is the major reason,

We will stay at home this season.

But when the sun shines in the spring,

We will be down to do our thing.

So when this nasty weather's gone,

For sure we will see you anon.

A note of regret to our friends Walt and Eileen McConville, for being unable to travel to Victoria for a Poetry Book event.

A POEM TO CHANGE

For evil to succeed, good men do naught,

Instead of doing what they really ought.

Bad deeds and evil come in many guises,

If we think about it, no surprises.

Bad deeds have mostly got the help they need,

Supported by hate, jealousy or greed.

And evil will always provide its share,

In secret or out in the public glare.

They could be mostly stopped before they start,

But men are oft too scared to do their part.

The fact, dear reader, is, if we believe,

All good men should be willing to concede.

I think that when they see this poem unfurled,

Enough good men could quickly change the world.

The best way for bad men to have success,

Is when good men continue to do less.

A SOBER THOUGHT

It's sad to think that something we enjoy,

Can be so detrimental and destroy

So many aspects of our daily lives,

Yet it continues to exist and thrives.

When first we taste an alcoholic drink,

We barely hesitate and do not think,

That such a pleasant taste and afterglow

Should have been greeted, not by "yes", but "no".

Just one glass there and another one here

It matters not if it's whiskey or beer.

The fact of the matter is that it's tough

To know you should stop when you've had enough.

So when you imbibe from this moment hence,

Just use your savvy and your commonsense.

You'll feel much better and a sense of joy

When you head for home as a sober boy.

I played trombone in a variety of dance-bands in Ireland, England and Canada. It provided me with an opportunity to observe the effect of "too much" alcohol on people. A little alcohol is fine, but drinking too much is extremely harmful to yourself and those around you. Know when to stop!

A TOAST TO THE LADIES

There are times throughout the year,

We honour those we hold so dear.

So here's to the ladies in our lives,

Our fond companions, friends and wives.

They give us strength like the Lord above,

Where would we be without their love?

Let's toast their health and never doubt them,

I'd hate to think of life without them.

So stand up tall and raise your glasses

And drink a toast to these lovely lasses

"TO THE LADIES!"

One evening at a very formal dinner in Port Hardy, the Chairman asked me would I please propose a Toast to the Ladies at the appropriate time. I said I would be delighted to comply with his request and wrote this poem on a table napkin.

Many of my friends have memorized it and use it whenever called upon to propose the Toast. It is dedicated to the Ladies and my Scottish pal, Scotty McLaren who was the first to memorize it.

A TRIBUTE TO BOB SWANSON, POET, INVENTOR, STEAM BUFF, LOGGER

A man of note, has left this earthly scene

From a life devoted, to control the God of Steam,

A genie hard to capture, hard to catch,

But in Bob Swanson, steam had met its match.

He started as a logger, to harvest Island hills,

And, at the hard knock 'Varsity', he soon acquired the skills

To help the gypo logger, reach his quota every day

And get enough logs harvested, to really make her pay.

In milling too, his sawmills worked so well

That stories of his talents, even bosses liked to tell.

But when the wood was loaded out, on train or logging truck,

And hauled down mountain inclines, for dumping in the chuck,

They lost some trucks and drivers, when brakes would give away,

So Bob was called by Government, to try to find a way

To design a braking system, that would safely do the job,

There was no one better qualified, than Engineering Bob.

His skills with valves and levers, acquired while handling steam

Were then applied to systems, achieving safety's dream.

He decided on a method, that no one else would dare,

He built a braking system, that would use compressed air.

Continued........

16

Continued………

It worked so very well, a technical success,

He was made the Head of Safety, Chief Inspector, no less.

And then the lure of steam, caught his interest once more

As diesel trains replaced, the steam train's strident roar.

The diesels were efficient, a wholly different sight

With a puny little warning horn, but no whistle in the night.

Bob studied all the whistle sounds, to find the perfect note,

And when the tests were ended, C Sharp received the vote.

It's eerie and plaintive, and its sounds will bring to mind

The magic of that era, that has now been left behind.

So when that lonesome whistle, comes piercing through the air,

Give thanks to Robert Swanson, who took the time to care.

His next big job was volunteering, skills to try bring back

The Royal Hudson engine, and place it on the track,

And just when people said, this project can't be done,

Bob donned his old blue coveralls, and made the hard work fun.

For members of his crew, who shared a common dream

To get the engine running with, a powerful head of steam.

And that's why steam train lovers, just tremble with delight

When they see the Royal Hudson, come puffing into sight.

Continued………

Continued.........

And when in '67, our great Centennial Year,

To celebrate our birthday, the Premier made it clear

The first notes of "O Canada" would be heard above the crowd,

Bob built a special whistle, to sound it strong and loud

Across Vancouver's rooftops, it's played each day at noon,

And people feel a certain pride, when they hear that Swanson tune.

Yes, Bob, was sure a man of note, in much more ways than one,

A poet, inventor, steam buff, a truly native son.

We were shocked and sad, when he passed away,

But Heaven has found, a bright new ray.

And in the logging camp, of the Holy Ghost

Somewhere along that heavenly coast

They'll give Bob Swanson, a first class bunk,

As the world's most famous whistle punk.

We were proud of you, as poet of the woods

In words and poems you captured the moods,

And from those of us who would dare to write,

We loved your poems, they were sheer delight.

So goodbye to you, old friend, old timer.

We'll never forget, such a great old rhymer.

In 1993, the Port McNeill Arts Alliance sponsored a memorable evening that featured Robert Swanson, the logger's poet, along with other fine performers. The Sunset School Gym was packed for that historical event, as poems and songs celebrated the rich history of our forest industry and the pioneering people who work in it.
Bob's poems were first published in little booklets with titles such as "Bunkhouse Ballads", "Rhymes of a Lumberjack", Rhymes of a Haywire Hooker" and Rhymes of a Western Logger". They are now available locally in one book entitled "Rhymes of a Western Logger". Bob Swanson passed away on the 4th of October 1994 at the age of 89. I went to the funeral service in Vancouver to pay my respects to a man who made me proud to be a logger. I had first read his poetry when I was a "bunkhouse guy" working for Pioneer Timber in Port McNeill in 1956.
This poem is my tribute to a great British Columbian, who was also proud to call himself a logger.

A TRIBUTE TO THE MASTER MECHANIC

The songs of the woods are the songs of the West
And the woods on the Coast are well known as the best.
The trees were the biggest, the territory rough,
To log them a logger just had to be tough.
This was no job for a big city dandy,
You had to be strong, really sharp and quite handy,
At falling and bucking and rigging the spars
And loading those logs on to trucks or rail cars.
The logs were then dumped at the beach in a boom
And rafted in sections 'til they ran out of room.
Now booming these logs required many skills
And tugboats for towing them down to the mills,
Where pulp and saw millers and some city mugs,
Not thinking too deeply, thought logs came from tugs,
Not giving a thought to the dangers that lurk,
Every day in the life of a logger at work.
We've come a long way and things have changed fast,
Since the first tree was cut and made into a mast.
And the sailors of yore who were men of the seas,
Settled ashore, became men of the trees,
Using windlass and drums as a logging machine,
Thankful for help from the Goddess of Steam,
Whose engines were famous as hardworking toilers
As long as they had lots of wood in their boilers.
Soon after Herr Diesel developed his oil
Some big diesel engines took over the toil.
Now we've heard that the logger was a man among men
But guess who became the main man among them?
The mechanic, his tools and his unending skills
Was behind every log that came out of the hills.
If motor or gear box ever ground to a stop,
A panicky call would be made to the Shop.
The message was clear, send us help, burn the dirt,
With the crew standing idle we're losing our shirt.

Continued ………

Continued.........

The Master Mechanic would say with a grin,

"It's time to help out those poor loggers ag'in."

And at night with each logger asleep in his bunk

The shop crews were working maintaining the junk.

We've heard that mechanics were men among men,

But it's time to revisit that concept again.

The boss of mechanics we know as the Master

Looks after the handling of every disaster.

The Master Mechanic's rule number one,

There is no such phrase, as "It can't be done".

When times are hard and the going is rough,

When ordinary men would have more than enough,

There's a true fact of life that we all know,

That's when the tough guys get ready to go.

When Master Mechanics go meet with St. Pete,

They'll not be sent down to the devil for heat,

Their God's sure to treat them especially well,

They've already spent a full lifetime in Hell.

Dedicated to my favourite Master Mechanic, Horace Arthurs.

While working as a chokerman for Pioneer Timber in 1956, I was fortunate to be involved in an accident between my right instep and a heavy choker bell on Twin Peaks Mountain. My foot swelled up and I could not wear my caulked boots.

I was given so-called "light-duty" work in the Repair Shop as I did not want to go on "Workers' Compensation". The Master Mechanic, Horace Arthurs, ran an efficient and spotless Repair Shop and liked to kid me about my Irish accent. He was a tough boss who had worked all over Coastal British Columbia and has since written a wonderful book called "The Last Wooden Spar" about his experiences as a pioneer logger.

His management method was unique in his ability to delegate and trust the men who worked in the shop and on the equipment out in the woods. He became my mentor and from him I learned a most important fact......there is no such phrase as "can't be done" in a mechanic's language.

AH, THOSE RULES

The rule when you're young and you're learning to think

Is that it is wrong to lie, steal, cheat or drink.

But as we mature and we first go to school,

We soon learn it's okay to ignore that rule.

It is not a sin if you LIE in the arms

Of the person you love, enthralled by their charms.

And it is not wrong if you just STEAL away

From any bad person you may meet today.

If you fall in the ocean, just hold your breath,

It's all right to CHEAT, when you are cheating death.

And should beauteous nature your passions foment

Just savour the fact and DRINK in the moment.

Regardless of how this rule is now spoken,

It's quite clear to me it's bound to be broken.

This poem has a moral. We shouldn't take things too literally in this life. Here are four words that say it's okay to Lie, Steal, Cheat and Drink.

One shouldn't jump to conclusions!

ALL THAT GLITTERS IS NOT GOLD

Lehman Brothers and A.I.G.

Came as quite a surprise to me.

They left their clients in the ditch,

While their bosses got filthy rich.

So hence this story being told,

The glitters do not mean it's gold.

The fact that these outfits went broke,

Is just another Wall Street joke.

They either dozed or even slept.

Their management was plain inept.

Of misery they've caused their share

Of damage, sadness and despair.

They should all be thrown into jail

And should be kept there without bail.

Indeed if it was up to me,

A hanging judge I'd have to be.

Jail sentences to instill awe,

I'd use the full power of the law.

Lehman Brothers and A.I.G. were two huge gilt-edged financial concerns that shocked everyone by running into major financial problems in 2008/09

"AN EARLY IMMIGRANT TO BRITISH COLUMBIA"

Our ship was just about a hundred feet,

One of the better ships within the fleet.

It had three masts to carry all the sails,

A crew of sixty, all of whom were males.

We headed out to sail the seven seas

And handled storms and headwinds with great ease.

When working on the sails we could not slip,

The rule, "one hand for self, one hand for ship."

The food was all hard tack and salted meat,

A stove below at midships supplied heat.

Avoiding scurvy was a job full-time,

'Twas treated with the bitter juice of lime.

One trip we made took us around Cape Horn,

It made me wonder just why I was born.

We tried to round it for a good five days,

Tough sailing, but our crew it did not faze.

Then Valparaiso was our port of call,

A miracle that we made port at all.

Our orders then were to sail further north,

A trip that we all hoped they'd soon abort.

We sailed on through the tropics and the heat

And came upon a land that smelled so sweet.

We sailed along its wild and rugged shore.

Its trees and mountains thrilled us to the core.

This land had been explored by ships from Spain.

They then moved on, they did not like the rain.

The British then laid claim to this great land,

Which made me make a move I had not planned.

I put all my belongings in a grip

And made the wild decision to jump ship.

AN ODE TO CHARLIE'S PLACE

The people of the Island North
Are surely the pioneering sort.
At times they need to travel South,
Which they describe as "getting out".
The road goes through a lonely land
Of verdant forest, stand by stand.
It's all the driver really sees,
`Tis the land of a trillion trees,
With hills and mountains, wildlife through,
Deer, elk and bears and cougars too.
It makes one think of no-mans-land,
A kind of desert without sand.
A desert needs a kind oasis
Which could describe what Charlie's Place is.
A breakfast, lunch and dinner place
You're bound to meet a friendly face.
In summer heat or winter snow,
Sayward Junction's the place to go.
It's where they feed the highway crews,
The place to get the highway news
And if the highway's blocked with snow
The Mounties will not let you go.
To your's and everyone's delight,
The place stays open through the night.
And if you need to use the phone
They'll let you call your folks at home.
You'll love the people's happy smiles
After driving those lonely miles.
Great food, good coffee, friendly faces,
The kind of stop that Charlie's Place is.

"Charlie's Place" was built at the Sayward Junction of the "new" Island Highway. It was named after Charlie Sacht by his daughter, Beverley. It was later purchased and operated by the Whites and later sold to Vicky and Laurie Landsdowne who were the owners when it shut down. Many North Islanders stopped there on their way up and down Island. It was a hospitable and welcoming stop in all seasons, but particularly in winter when the snow got too bad to face the Sayward Hill and the hundred miles of wilderness country to Port Hardy.

AN ODE TO KEVIN FALCON

The news for many years has been,

About the anti-logging scene.

It's also, sadly, been about,

The efforts to keep mining out.

And protesters of every hue

Have wiped out jobs at fish farms too.

These "folks" are shameless when they boast,

About their efforts on this coast.

They rant and constantly they vent,

On Minister, Environment,

And also subject to this zoo,

The Minister of Forests too.

The Minister of Highways now,

Is facing problems 'bout the brow

Of hillside over in West Van.,

Where citizens say if you can,

Avoid a highway o'er the bluff;

A tunnel would be good enough.

They posed for pictures in the buff,

Their privates covered with some fluff,

Which on that rocky ground was tough,

Proving they're made of stronger stuff.

They do not like K. Falcon's guff,

So now they're camping in the rough.

Continued........

Continued………

At least they've gotten off their duff

And made poor Kevin huff and puff.

But sadly they must deep down know,

A tunnel's not the way to go.

The cost is astronomical,

Their protest somewhat comical.

The cost of building "Sea to Sky"

Is definitely much too high.

It's time to now, relax, relent,

Appreciate this Government.

Give credit to young Kevin too,

He did the only thing to do.

There was great controversy in West Vancouver over the design of the "Sea to Sky" highway near Horseshoe Bay on the way to Whistler. The burghers of West Vancouver campaigned in typical "anti-development" fashion. They even got some brave souls to pose in the nude for a magnificent black and white calendar. The Minister of Highways held to the "high ground" in the interest of avoiding a costly tunnel underneath the mountainside. Commonsense prevailed in the interests of the provincial taxpayer. Highways Minister Kevin Falcon made the right decision and I like to think that my poem, which he graciously acknowledged, lightened his load.

ASPIRATIONS!

Each one amongst us has the worthy aim

And in this way we're really all the same.

We work hard as we strive for each success,

Accepting all the pressures and the stress.

In some ways such success is rather nice

But melts away just like the late spring ice.

Along with our success there comes respect,

A prize that few of us would e'er reject.

But there's a higher prize that I desire,

A sky-high level to which I aspire.

I'm hoping to become the kind of man

That my old dog at home thinks that I am.

Dedicated to dog lovers everywhere.

BACK TO CAMP

He may have been a farmer's boy
A' working on the land,
Or maybe worked a fish boat job,
A life at sea so grand.
Perhaps he worked at labour hard,
A diggin' in the muck,
Or thought that he might have more fun
If he was driving truck.
And for myself I have to say
I've tried each of these jobs
And don't know what it would be like
To join the suited mobs,
Who work at office jobs in Town
Succeed by kissing bums,
I think I'll stay right where I am
And wait and see what comes.

Two loggers splicing a wire cable, using marlin spikes.
By Heather Brown

Dedicated to every regular guy who signed on to be a logger in a Coastal logging camp, and decided to stay the course.

BE AWARE

Our ancestors in days of old

Took pride in strength and being bold.

These traits were passed down thru the years

And helped to obviate the fears

That would most likely start to haunt

Their warriors' minds and even daunt

The bravest of their fighting men

Should they be faced with war again.

The leaders of these men, we know,

All liked to have their own motto.

The concept was it would inspire,

Avoiding consequences dire.

With words like "VICTORY" and "STRENGTH".

These men would go to any length.

They'd win the fight at any cost,

Those with the weakest motto lost.

Good mottoes still today abound,

The best of all can still be found,

In words of every Guide and Scout,

Just "Be prepared" before going out.

But for myself I really care

For my own motto "Be aware".

It's comprehensive and the best

Because it covers all the rest.

Mottoes have always intrigued me. They give us something to live up to.

A TICKET ON THE S.S. CATALA (JUNE 1956)

The chalkboard in the window said it all

Come in, this is the Logger's hiring hall.

We're hiring for our camps along the Coast,

Alaska Pine would like to be your host,

The Union steamship sails tomorrow night

We need some husky loggers sharp and bright.

So if you'll sign along this dotted line

You'll be among the finest of the fine.

We only log in daylight not in dark

And where we log is much like Stanley Park,

So if it's fame and fortune that you seek

We hope you'll stay for more than just a week.

We're sending you to work in Port McNeill

It's just the kind of place that makes you feel

That if you really want to learn to log

And you are not inclined to duck the fog,

You might stay 'round and get to know the ropes

And see how loggers log those forest slopes.

You'll need a hardhat, Stanfields and caulk boots,

In case it rains, one of them slicker suits.

This prepaid ticket lets you board the ship

You'll embark at the Union Steamship slip.

You've got yourself a one-way ticket cruise

And a special way of life, you cannot lose.

Now as you leave this useless city strife

And take your first steps to a logger's life

Continued………

Continued.........

There's a fifty-fifty chance you'll stay the course

And if you do you'll surely be a force,

So work hard and get used to doing things right

And heed some sage advice, "stay outta the bight".

On Saturday night at about six o'clock,

We made our way down to the old steamship dock.

Ready for all that the future might bring,

Two simple greenhorns not knowing a thing.

The ship's crew was hustling and loading on freight

While taxis were dropping folks off at the gate.

A mixture of loggers, some young and some old

With one thing in common, they'd all spent their gold,

Sure that they'd had the best time of their lives

While bidding adieu to their girlfriends and wives.

As soon as the crowd was all ushered aboard

The whistle was sounded, the gangplank was lowered.

The S.S. Catala with its victims of fate

Sailed into the sunset out through the Lion's Gate.

A supper was served on tablecloths white

As she sailed north on that fine summer night.

After the supper we heard the good news,

Party in Bull-pen, with all kinds of booze.

So down we went to the bowels of the ship

Wanting to prove to them all we were hip.

We soon became part of the noise and the din,

Baptized by new friends with beer, whiskey and gin.

Continued.........

Continued………

So that's how we spent our first night on the Coast

And woke to a breakfast, eggs, bacon and toast.

Soon after the ship blew its whistle in warning

And made Kelsey Bay the first stop of the morning.

Then into Port Neville to drop off more freight

Before heading west to traverse Johnstone Strait.

Telegraph Cove was the next place to stop

Where some of the locals came on board to shop.

Then tooting its horn, the ship gracefully hove

Around the rock bluff into Beaver Cove,

Where Elephant Mountain so regally looms

Over the bay with its acres of booms.

Then to Alert Bay, a cute little town

Where from the hillside, some totems look down.

Then off we sailed to the Port of McNeill

In time to sit down to a fabulous meal.

The cook and his helpers had done themselves proud

In feeding good food to a big motley crowd.

Then off to the office, once we were fed

Where we were assigned to a bunkhouse and bed.

And at the dawn of the following morn

We woke to the sound of a god-awful horn.

Breakfast was served, the gut-hammer ringing

Our life in the woods was only beginning….

………more……….

DAYLIGHT IN THE SWAMPS

We ate a big breakfast and made up our lunch,

Then off to the yard with the rest of the bunch.

A line up of crummies, a dozen or so,

With engines a warming being readied to go.

A foreman was striding around in the crowd

Barking out orders in a voice that was loud.

Slowly but surely we were all sorted out,

Not knowing what any of this was about.

My buddy and I were assigned to a bus,

The driver of which was a logger called Russ.

Now this was the bus of the Big Skidder crew,

A tough bunch of loggers who knew what to do.

They logged with a skyline, the slopes of Twin Peaks

And all liked to joke we'd be done in three weeks.

A big wooden spar tree stood tall by the road,

This held the skyline and the hayrack to load,

The trucks and their trailers that hauled out the logs,

Being loaded by loaders who just worked like dogs.

The skyline stretched up to the top of the hill

The thought of going up there almost made us ill.

Then Carl, our foreman, the boss of this show,

Said, "climb up that sidehill until you reach snow.

Continued........

Continued.........

You'll see that the skyline is anchored to stumps

Enabling the logs hauled to miss all the humps.

But now we must move it along to the west

This means we need new stumps to anchor it best."

We started to climb with back-rigger McLean

And two other greenhorns, a Finn and a Dane.

We climbed and we hustled the rest of the day,

Impressed by how hard loggers worked for their pay.

Our lunch was sent out on the skyline at noon

And quitting time could not come for us too soon.

So back to the Camp for a shower and a feed,

Then straight to our bunks, we were too tired to read.

Each day we went out we would learn something new

And soon became part of the permanent crew.

The trees were all felled by men skilled in falling,

Working with power saws, a most dangerous calling.

The roads through the woods were built by a few

Cat skinners, rock blasters, a foreman named Stu.

The yarding and loading was done by a crew

Hooker, rigging slinger, three chokermen too.

The boss of these loggers, a guy named Art Lowe

Drove 'round like a whirlwind, always on the go.

Continued.........

Continued………

The logs were all hauled to the spar by the road,

Where the logging trucks came to pick up their load.

A loading-pot lifted the logs on each truck

With tongs swung by loaders who lived by sheer luck.

Then to the salt chuck to the logging truck dump

Where they unloaded with a god-awful thump.

The logs were then rafted, towed out by a tug,

Dark brown on the water, a two-acre rug.

These log booms became the life-blood of the mills,

Where workers think naught of our life in the hills.

The wealth of our province, oft taken for granted

Relies very much on what nature has planted.

We could not afford all the things that we need,

If our great province was not so well treed.

And so as we toiled in the woods every day

I soon realized I was destined to stay,

Though often to test us our mates took a shot

Which forced us to give just as good as we got.

I'm happy to say that I have no regrets

This life in B.C. is a good as it gets.

Continued………

Continued.........

In May 1956, my childhood friend, Tom Murphy, and I emigrated to Canada. After a series of adventures working in London for two years and hitch-hiking around Europe and the Eastern United States we found ourselves in Vancouver, British Columbia. We saw logging jobs advertised in the window of the Alaska Pine and Cellulose Company on Pender Street. As we had just driven two convertibles across the States from Toronto to Vancouver for a car-dealer, we applied for jobs as "logging truck drivers". The man behind the counter asked us where we had driven logging trucks and we told him, in Ireland. Satisfied that we were greenhorns, he signed us up as "chokermen", gave us two tickets and told us to board the S.S. Catala on the Union Steamship dock at seven o'clock on Saturday night. Hence, the two poems about becoming loggers.

A small steamship, the S/S Catala, made two trips up the West Coast every week, carrying supplies, food, parts and people returning to their homes and workplaces along the barely inhabited Coast. Leaving a city like London with its eight million people and having hitch-hiked through large European cities, Vancouver was like a big town, no high-rises, no Skytrain, no Seabus and a big Chinatown.

The Sylvia Hotel at English Bay, had a great restaurant on an upper floor (the fifth or sixth) and advertised it as "Dine in the Sky". Hyperbole at its best. Its hyperbole, has served the city well. I have borrowed some for our Town as it has grown from a basic bunkhouse Logging Camp of about two hundred people, to the nice rounded Town of three thousand people that it is today. Our logging camp became a Village Municipality on 18 February 1966 and became the FIRST town incorporated in Canada on the day that Her Majesty Queen Elizabeth signed Canada's own Constitution on 17th April 1987.

Our Premier at the time was the Honourable Bill Bennett and the Minister of Municipal Affairs was the Honourable Bill van der Zalm. His Honour, "Budge" Bell Irving was the Lieutenant Governor who graciously waited until Her Majesty signed, before he signed the order in Council creating the Town of Port McNeill.

BEREFT

The crumbling farmhouse sits atop the hill
The yard and sheds around it, quiet and still.
The river gurgles on its way below,
Beside the river meadows, flowing slow.
That pleasant murmur is the only sound
To break the silence of the fields around.
Where once the baa of sheep would have been heard,
With farmyard lowing of the dairy herd.
The place is now devoid of any noise,
No longer heard, the playing girls and boys,
Who long have left this pastoral abode
To take up other roles on life's long road.
The milking shed, the heart of every farm,
Has long lost all its very special charm,
Where each cow stood and waited for her turn,
Contributing rich milk to each day's churn.
The orchard with its ancient apple trees
Once produced crops of fruit with fertile ease.
The kitchen garden filled the family's needs,
Is sadly covered now with crops of weeds.
The farmer and his wife gone to their rest,
A proud long life, in which they gave their best.
Their grave beside the church is all that's left,
The village, farm and family, now bereft.

Small farms were the backbone of the Irish countryside and the Irish economy. With modern farming methods, many small farms have been amalgamated in the interest of economy and efficiency. It is sad to see many of them around the Irish Countryside being farmed by large corporations and the houses and farm buildings lying idle. This poem is about a farm near Glanworth in County Cork, where I lived at one time.

BOOMERANG

It is not wise to criticize

Our friends who make mistakes,

But it's the truth and fact to boot,

It but a moment takes.

It's also true it could be you

Who's next to take a hit.

So let us dare to show we care

And make the best of it.

Just keep in mind we should be kind

When next a friend's in trouble,

For if you had, you'll be so glad,

Should trouble backwards double.

Here is a poetic reminder to anyone who may be inclined to deride a friend or acquaintance that has screwed up. It could be your turn next, in which you may need a word of encouragement or a helping hand. We reap what we sow.

BUNKHOUSE LIFE

Life in a bunkhouse can be quite a strain,
I would not want to go through it again.
Monday to Friday was quite bad enough,
With working long hours, it was fairly tough.
Saturday, Sunday were really much worse,
Boredom on those days was really a curse.
A camp full of men, with most of them broke,
Trying to save up for a wintertime "poke".
Had to stay out of the camp poker shack
Where you could not find an unmarked card pack.
Some would break down and speedboat to the Bay.
Where it was easy to spend all your pay.
Some did their laundry, took time for a walk,
With polyglot room-mates, much interesting talk.
Learn about places that you've never seen,
Tell about places where you may have been.
Learn about all sorts of places elsewhere,
Of customs and countries with people from there.
Oil up your caulk boots, replace worn spikes,
Talk about loggers and other folks psyches.
Afternoon Sunday there was an event
That eased the boredom of each bunkhouse gent.
The passenger ship arrives at the dock,
Close to the Camp, a five minute walk.
Check if the new-hires are men of renown,
Say our good-byes to those headed for Town.
Then back to Camp with a big appetite,
Best meal of the week was on Sunday night.
Then to the bunkhouse, get ready for bed,
Get a good sleep for the tough week ahead.

Dedicated to all those great loggers who signed out "tough". As there were few permanent communities along the Coast and virtually no roads, the logging companies had to create their own Camps with bunkhouses, a Cookhouse, Workshop, with Warehouse and a Commissary for basic needs like gloves, rain clothes, hard-hats, tobacco and snoose.

(Photo by Stu Crabe)Courtesy of West Coast Helicopters

An aerial view of modern-day Port McNeill showing town subdivisions encircling the centrally located schools, playing fields and recreation facilities that have been developed in recent years. Log-booming in distance at head of the bay.

An early view of Port McNeill circa 1940. Note "fore & aft" road built on pilings, encircling the bunkhouses, cookhouse, workshop and booming grounds.

"CANDY IS DANDY, BUT LIQUOR IS QUICKER".

According to old Ogden Nash,

There is no point in offering cash.

He's well aware that giving flowers

Will likely take too many hours.

Should you ever want to risk it,

It will take more than a biscuit.

He feels that if your mood is randy,

You're likely to succeed with candy

But then concludes that if in doubt,

It's time to get the liquor out.

You surely will achieve success,

Make sure you're at the right address.

The title of this little poem was inspired by the famous quote of the great American humourist, OGDEN NASH 1902/1971

CAN TWO BITS OF DUST MAKE THREE?

Our glimpse of life is sadly all too brief,

'Til death comes unannounced, just like a thief.

We do not know the year, the day, the hour,

Forestalling it is far beyond our power.

We're born and never really know the why,

Yet from the start we know we're going to die.

The challenge is for each of us the same,

To recognize we're pawns in Someone's game,

A puzzle to which each of us gives thought,

A question on which often wars are fought.

A man called Darwin tried his very best,

But his evolution theory fails the test.

His theory was that man evolved from dust,

But Who supplied the procreative lust?

I have listened to many people over the years talking about God, and while I am not sure as to who or what God is, I am totally awed by Nature in all its forms. I don't believe that all of these wonderful things just happened. There had to be a guiding hand to create the wonders and varieties of fish, animals, insects, birds, flowers, trees and humans. Just the magic of a caterpillar becoming a butterfly is enough for me to believe in a Supreme Being. And that's just a tiny example. Darwin's theory of evolution is fine, but he could not tell us who supplied the procreative lust. I dedicate this poem to all similar believers.

CARPE DIEM OR SEIZE THE DAY

Once in a while,
There's times when I'll
Think of some subject new,
And make a note,
It's time I wrote,
`Bout someone just like you.
Now some are glad
And some are mad
When they see their name in print,
But I don't care
If they despair
So I hope they'll take a hint.
That I must write
When the time is right
Or the world will miss the chance,
To get a look
At this little book
And think it's worth a glance.
So if you read
This little bead
Of warning, here up front,
You can't accuse
This cheeky muse
Of not being fairly blunt.
In fact it's fair,
I do declare
I call them as I see `em.
But I follow the rule
Of the writer's school
And always carpe diem.

I have always liked the phrase "Carpe diem", which I first learnt during Latin class. The lesson is, of course, that we should appreciate each day and make the most of it, so Carpe Diem!

CARRYING ON

It's been a few weeks now,
But his presence is everywhere.
As the first rays of daylight
Glint through the bedroom curtains,
She wakes and reaches out
To his side of the bed.
It's cold.
Cold as the realization
That he is not there anymore.
His masculine presence is still there,
In every corner of the room,
In every corner of the house.
His clothes and boots
Are still in the cupboard.
The essence of his manly presence
Still hangs in the air,
Reassuringly.
It's everywhere in the house,
Always was, always will be.
From his seat at the kitchen counter
To his tool-box in the car-port.
And his Harley, his pride,
Beside his self-built bike
That took so long to build.
Her mind goes back
To her part-time after-school job
At the local Shell Gas Station.
Hot summer days in tee-shirt
And tight jean shorts.
The roar of a Harley
Pulling up to the pumps.

Continued........

Continued………

"Dawn, you have a customer"
Said Bill the Manager.
She raced to the pumps,
"Fill`er up" said the biker.
"And would you like your windows cleaned?"
Said she.
He laughed.
She liked this tough-looking
Curly-headed stranger
With the twinkle in his eye
And a lamb at heart.
"Is there any place a guy can get a beer `round here?"
"Lots of places, well one for sure" said she.
"It's just a little town."
After her shift they went for a hamburger,
Their first meal together.
The first of many.
Then two great reliable and attentive kids,
And more recently a lovely grandchild.
Then a sudden sickness,
Incurable.
Constant visits by caring friends and family,
His passing in the local hospital.
And the largest attendance ever seen
At a funeral service in our Town.
The whole town came to say good-by,
A send-off he well deserved.

Dedicated to my long-term friend Dawn Harilstad and her family, on the passing of her husband, Mel.

CAULK BOOTS (I)

It's sad that men in fancy suits

Don't know too much about caulk boots,

Except for those who used to work

In logging jobs where dangers lurk.

Those are the folk who understand

The challenge working forest land.

Where slip'ry slopes control your speed,

You quickly realize you need

The kind of boots with spiky soles,

As loggers carry out their roles,

When falling, bucking, loading out,

Production's what it's all about.

When they wear out, replace each spike

And they will grip, the way you like.

So take good care of your caulk boots,

A first-class logger to your roots.

Please keep them oiled, well polished too

And they will take good care of you.

CAULK BOOTS (II)

Caulk boots
The proud badge of a logger.
Indispensable.
The only safe footwear
For those who would conquer the forest
In the battles for wood.
Climbing the side-hills,
Clambering over stumps and logs,
Crushing the salal
And stomping the devil's club.
They made it possible for the logger
To work safely,
In one of the most demanding,
Dangerous jobs anywhere.
The best boots were made in Vancouver
By the Pierre Paris Company.
The Sunday routine in Camp
Was to spend the time
Oiling and polishing the boots,
Checking the sharpness of the spikes
And replacing them if necessary
In gratitude for keeping us,
Uninjured and alive.
The fallers, rigging crews
And the dancing boom crew
Balancing on slippery logs in the booming grounds
Could not survive without them.
They pronounced caulk as Cork
But I never questioned it.
After all, it reminded me of the people of my hometown,
Cork, Ireland
Tough and reliable.

The well worn caulk boots of Mickey Brown.

From a black and white drawing by the artist Heather Brown.

CEDAR TEA

If you should suffer pains and aches,

There is a cure, here's what it takes,

Check out a nearby Cedar tree

And pick some green twigs to make tea.

A goodly fistful of these tips

Will make great tea to wet your lips.

Now put them in a good-sized pot.

Two pints of water boiling hot.

Now simmer it for half an hour,

Then strain the liquid, its got power.

You drink it hot, or drink it cold.

It's really worth its weight in gold.

Your pains and aches will disappear,

There's no more pain pills needed here.

Good for any pains that ail you

This great tea just will not fail you.

So now to give yourself the edge

Just find yourself a Cedar hedge

Dedicated to Clem Ruel, a North Island logger who told me of the wonders of cedar tea.

CORK'S MOST FAMOUS PUB

A warm muggy day.
Mail two letters at the Main Post Office,
'Tis mid-afternoon
And after standing in a queue to buy stamps,
I step out into Oliver Plunket Street.
The muggy heat is having an effect
And there's a need for relief.
Out of the corner of my eye,
That knowing right eye,
I spot the cure, across the street.
'Tis the Hi B,
In all of its Cork finery.
I climb the stairs to the best-known upstairs pub
In all of Ireland.
The stairs service a few other businesses as well,
Stumble in the door off the first landing.
More muggy air, but with a flavour.
There's a rugby-scrum of fans
Crowded around the bar,
Behind which, is Esther, drawing pints,
Chatting to the admiring scrum,
Under the watchful eye of our host
The infamously famous Brian O'Donnell, owner,
Cork's best-known publican,
Host, jazz fan, artist, raconteur,
And old school-friend.
The low ceiling gives the room
A down-to-earth intimacy
Emphasized by the welcoming Esther,
Who greets regulars and irregulars with a sincere,
"How are you, luv?"

Continued........

Continued ……..

She draws the requested creamy-topped pint of nectar,
Courtesy of Arthur Guinness and his age-old company.
Passed over their heads by members of the counter scrum,
"She said you can pay later," says the scrum half,
As he placed the glass reverentially on my table.
It's time to sit back and relax
In the warm, acceptably warm, atmosphere.
My seat by the door
Is fanned by the openings and closings
As the patrons go in and out for a smoke.
Also time to recognise the life-like portraits
That line the walls,
Drawn by a pre-publican Brian,
And signed personally for him by his subjects
Clark Gable, Bing Crosby, Somerset Maugham, Eamonn De Valera,
Albert Einstein, Cecil B de Mille, Sir Alexander Fleming,
The scientist who discovered penicillin,
And many others, in this unique portrait gallery.
The philosophy of the establishment is spelled out
In a sign behind Esther,
As she draws those unending pints……
"If you're drinking to forget,
Please pay in advance."
As Esther draws yet another pint
While chatting away to her admiring fans,
I'm reminded of a line
From Oliver Goldsmith's, "The Deserted Village,"
"And still they gazed and still the wonder grew,
At all the pints of Guinness that she drew."

One of the most unique pubs in a land and city of unique pubs, the Hi B (pronounced Hy Bee) is well worth a visit. Its owner is, among other attributes, a fabulous artist. As a young man he drew amazingly accurate portraits of many famous people and sent them to his subjects to be autographed. The subjects were obviously impressed because they signed without demur. I hope that you will be able to visit while Esther is still charming the scrum around the Bar.

DARLING, IF ONLY I KNEW

By Brian Zak

Darling, if only I knew what I know now,

Life for our family would likely have been different.

I would not have taken so much for granted

My focus in life would have been less materialistic.

In being the Father I had set my priorities

To reflect what I thought was important and valued.

In looking around now, those things sure look different

I was blind I am certain to what really counted.

If only I knew that you'd leave us so early

My love for you and Tif would have come out so different.

I wouldn't have said no, or at least not as often

And in saying yes, our times together would not have been so short.

If only I knew this pain was forthcoming

I would have ensured our talks to be different.

My patience towards you would have been extended much longer

My anger at times would have been less severe.

Continued………

Continued.........

To only be your father, for a short 17 years

Seems to be unfair, unjust and oh so very painful

There's so many things that I'd like to change

And so many words I wish I could take back.

Darling, If only I knew I would have tried different

To show you my love in so many ways.

Words can't express my love or my sorrow

I really do wish now it could have been better.

I know you're now safe, at peace and in heaven

But you will be with us forever in our hearts and our minds

There will be a time, when we're together as a family

In heaven with you, where all dreams come true.

My darling Larisa, if only I knew.......

Love Dad

April 5, 1993

My friend Brian Zak wrote this beautiful poem after his seventeen year old daughter, Larisa, died in a car accident. His poem so impressed me that I asked his permission to include it in my book. Every parent will understand the poignancy of this heartfelt poem.

DRIVING, THINKING, WRITING

I do a lot of thinking when I drive,

It keeps me wide awake and mind alive.

And on the seat beside me is a pad

Of writing paper, yes, I know it's bad.

But if I get a new poetic thought,

I do what I must do, it's what I ought.

I put my pen to work and write it out,

It makes the trip go fast, without a doubt.

While driving I just cannot watch my pen

Oft` times I'll write across a line again,

Which often leaves me with a wordy mess,

Interpretations later made by guess,

Some of the poems within this little book

Were written as I drove and could not look.

I had to do it, dangerous to be sure,

It's my attempt at highway literature.

Port McNeill is near the north end of Vancouver Island. My work often requires me to drive to Campbell River (200km), to Nanaimo (350km), to Port Alberni (350km) and Victoria (500km). My wife can't always get away to accompany me, so I am often alone, with time to think. A great time to write.(see poem "To Mark")

DYNAMITE

A down-to-earth old logging camp,
With cold winter weather so damp.
A night to be in from the cold,
With great B.S. stories being told.
The pot-bellied stove was a treat,
It gave off such comforting heat.
And sitting around were the crew,
The bulk of them pot-bellied too.
Old Rocky the blaster told tales
On the years he spent riding the rails.
And then he described dynamite
And said that 'twas easy to light.
Powder sticks burned just like wood,
For lighting fires, were just as good.
A young lad we just knew as Pat,
Said, "I just do not believe that."
Slipped out the door, said, "I'll be back.
Gone for sticks from the powder shack."
Came back with four sticks in his hand
And close by the stove took a stand.
Old Rocky with face turning white,
Said "Careful, that is dynamite.
Being careless with that stuff is dumb,
Could blow us all to kingdom come."
Said Pat, "I'll throw them in the stove
To see if they will burn, by Jove."
And as he bent to throw them in,
Old Rocky made an awful din
"I stand for this madness no more."
He was the first man out the door.

This poem is based on a talk with Pat Brown who was the Pat in this poem. The blaster was bravely telling the crew that they used to use sticks of dynamite to light fires at lunchtime to toast their sandwiches.

EARLY SHIFT

If steady work is what you seek
There's forty work hours in a week.
A normal shift, eight hours a day
That's what you need to make 'er pay.
For most of us we rise and shine
We're all at work by eight or nine.
There's some who go to work at night
And work by moon, see no sunlight.
Then there's a shift, oh joy of joys,
To separate the men from boys.
It happens in the summer heat
And forest fire it's used to beat.
So, when the woods are powder dry,
We rise at three, I do not lie.

The breakfast served before the dawn
Gulped down fast with many a yawn.
Then to the woods on early shift,
Extra money, time and a fifth.
The engines warmed up before five,
Air cool and clear, we felt alive.
And by the time the clock struck one,
Eight loads of logs, our work was done.
Sit in the crew-bus start to snore
Before the driver shuts the door.
Then back to camp, a wash, a shower,
With three o'clock the dinner hour.
By six we hit the sack again
And pray to God to send us rain.

Work schedules in logging camps were often changed during "fire season", as it was safer to log early in the morning in order to avoid the hottest time of the day.

'ECTION 15

What a collection.

Great intellection.

Like the direction.

Quite a confection.

Almost perfection.

Had an inspection.

Slight imperfection.

Needs a correction.

After detection.

Under reflection.

No further dissection.

Poet's election.

Head of the section.

My predilection.

And my affection.

A poem that I sent to acknowledge a great collection of new poems by my friend Walt McConville.

ENOUGH ALREADY

I've had a great few weeks in town,

No shortage of great fun.

But now it's time, so back to work

And leave that special one.

Oh she was pleased to spend the time

And almost all my cash,

A party almost every night

And on weekends, a bash.

So I am heading back to Camp

and leaving her behind,

A much more thoughtful sober me.

How could I be so blind?

Written for a lot of my friends who regularly went to Vancouver when they thought they had too much money saved, up.

FOR WHOM THE BELL TOLLS

by

John Donne

No man is an island entire of itself.

Every man is a piece of the continent,

A part of the main.

If a clod be washed away by the sea,

Europe is the less.

As well as if a promontory were,

As well as if a mansion of thy friend's,

Or of thine own, were.

Every man's death diminishes me,

Because I am involved in mankind.

And therefore, never send to know

For whom the bell tolls.

It tolls for thee.

*"For whom the bell tolls" is one of the best known poems in the English language.
My riposte to it is on the following page.*

EVERY MAN IS AN ISLAND

The concept that no man is an island,

Writ by someone in pie-in-the-sky-land.

It may have been a worthy thought back then,

But it is time to look at it again.

John Donne was writing in much simpler times

When serious thoughts were oft described in rhymes.

But it is time to challenge his great verse,

To leave such thoughts unchallenged would be worse.

It may have been appropriate at the time

To publicize the Ruler's party-line,

That every man is treated much the same,

As he, each day, takes part in this life's game.

John Donne ignored the fact that men were slaves,

That Kings and Lords were often worse than knaves.

'Tis really difficult to state this fact,

To question such a writer requires tact.

The sad truth is that each man's on his own

And should be honoured in a special poem.

Each man can only count upon himself,

As he goes out each day to earn his pelf.

So, yes, the bell should always daily toll

To honour each man reaching for his goal.

Admirers of John Donne (1572-1631) may not agree with my thoughts on the great poet and priest. He was of Welsh extraction and led a favoured life. It was easy for him to assert that "no man is an island", but the vast majority of men had to stand alone as a human island, and, still do.

FOLLOW THE MONEY

Of pressure groups I've had my fill,

Regurgitating, as they will.

Pouring out their doom and gloom

To such extent there is no room

For commonsense or fair debate,

It's their way, or they can't relate

To those amongst us who must work

To answer each and every quirk

That they put on the planning table

Which is how they are so able

To wipe out jobs that harvest wood

And shut down mining when they could.

Fish farms too are now in danger,

To this pressure they're no stranger.

This whole movement is so spooky

People that eat too much sushi.

These careless types, well-spoken too,

An anti-economic crew

Drawn like bees to a hive of honey

And all that free Foundation money.

Each could be called a headline hogger,

Which makes me want to hug a logger.

I'm also told there's nothing finer

Than to hug a working miner,

And you just ain't seen nothing yet,

'Til an aquaculture hug you get.

Continued.........

Continued.........

So now these unproductive folk

Regard our efforts as a joke.

They're honing in on oil and gas

While we hoped they would let it pass.

Our health and welfare and our schools

Are being affected by these fools.

Ten years of government being rash

Have left our province short of cash.

We need more money in our coffers

And the wealth industry offers.

Let's hope these ENGOS and their crew

Will find more useful things to do.

And maybe from this moment hence

They'll all be blessed with commonsense.

British Columbia has often been likened to California. As such, it has attracted many people who have no idea as to how an economy works, especially a resource-dependent economy like ours in British Columbia.. Our province covers a very large chunk of North America. It is an expensive place to service a population of about three million. Most of the population is concentrated in the South Westerly corner and the balance of the population is spread all over the province in little towns and villages, many of them hundreds of miles apart. Expensive highways, bridges and infrastructure are needed. Some wealthy U.S. Foundations have been financing campaigns to shut down some of our most important industries. Forestry, Mining, Aquaculture and Power Generation have all been attacked in the name of "environmentalism".

FOOTSTEPS IN THE DARK

If you work nights, alone, outdoors,

Especially outdoors,

You become attuned to the dark,

The shadows, the silence,

And the loneliness.

A cold, rainy, late November night,

My shift is finished,

The oil barge cast off,

The dock lights are switched off.

I close and lock the pipeline and tank valves

And walk in pitch darkness

Up the gravel roadway towards my truck.

Suddenly, footsteps behind me,

The sound of loose gravel being kicked,

By a heavy foot.

Hair standing up on the back of my neck

And a shiver of primal fear runs up my spine.

Reach my truck, jump in, slam door,

Switch on headlights,

And stare into the implacable big round eyes

Of Bob Coté's cow.

I've spent many nights on top of the big fuel tanks in our bulk oil plant at Beach Camp, Port McNeill, as oil tankers pumped petroleum products ashore.

One of our pioneering neighbours, Bob Coté, had bought some cows which he planned to move to an area he was planning to homestead outside of town. In the meantime he was keeping them near his mobile home, not too far from our bulk plant.

FROM A FAN

The hockey season's just begun,

A chance for you to have some fun.

Appreciate your parents who

Put so much time and effort too.

To get you to the hockey rink,

It's not as easy as you think.

You learnt a lot at hockey school

And most important was the rule

To show respect for every player,

No matter what, always play fair.

Please pay attention to your coach

As he/she may have a new approach

To teaching you to play the game,

Not many coaches are the same,

And as you play the season through

There'll be some pressures placed on you.

There's sometimes folks outside the glass

Who shout if you should miss a pass.

There's others who may scream and yell,

They think this is the NHL.

These idiots who loudly bray,

Did not play hockey in their day,

Continued........

Continued.........

For if they had they'd understand

The pressures and the sheer demand

On every player on these teams,

With some not even in their teens.

Enjoy the game for all our sakes,

Regardless of the time it takes.

The challenge is to do your best.

You're having fun, that is the test.

We all enjoy it when we win

But losing is not such a sin.

As long as you enjoy the game,

To win or lose it's all the same.

So pay attention, keep in mind,

Just keep your cool, be firm, be kind.

A logging camp Manager named Dale Chilton spear-headed the building of an ice arena in Port McNeill. Our arena has produced some great hockey players such as N.H.L. defenceman Willie Mitchell who has been a great model as a hockey player and an inspiration to all the young people of our community. This poem is written to remind young players to enjoy themselves and have fun playing the game.

FULL MOON AT INCHYDONEY

Along the beach outside this great hotel,

I walk alone and watch the tidal swell.

The sands feel warm and pleasant at my feet,

The midnight air of Inchydoney, sweet.

Each wave rolls gently in along the sand,

Stirred up far out to sea by nature's hand.

The force that sends these waves across the sea,

Intrigue and raise my curiosity,

For that same ocean sends each rolling wave

To every shore that it's great waters have.

The waves that hit these shores come from the West,

They've rolled to Irish shores to seek their rest.

Yet other waves have flowed the other way

And landed on the shores of the U.S.A.

These waves roll North and also to the South

To meet Pacific waves and fight it out.

For me there is an over-riding riddle

Just who stirs up these waves out in the middle?

And then I see a light from out the gloom

It is the face of gravity, the Moon.

And as it looks across that lunar mile

Its face takes on a mischief-laden smile

It could a smile of knowing-mischief be,

Or even just a smile of luna-sea.

Written at midnight during a walk under a full moon, on the sands of Inchydoney, near Clonakilty, Co. Cork.

HENRY NEWTON SMITH

A TRIBUTE

This poem is written to honour one of my best friends, on the occasion of his seventieth birthday. Harry Smith was one of the Trail Smokeaters when they won the World Cup in 1961. He went on to run different businesses and has retired two or three times, but is still working. This is a tribute to a great all 'round guy, my friend, Harry Smith, founding President of Columbia Fuels.

Trail Smokeaters – 1961 World Champions

Top row - l to r Eric Hewitt (vice pres.), Gordon Sharp (dir), Don Matheson (dir), Ed Cristofoli, George Ferguson, Darryl Sly, Dr. Jack Colbert (team doctor), Bruce Hogle (dir), James Cameron (pres).
Middle row - Harry Smith, Cal Hockley, Don Fletcher, Harold Jones, Frank Turik, Dave Rusnell, Walt Peacosh, Joe Garay (trainer), Ugo DeBiasio, (mgr,secy treas.).
Front row - Marshall Anselmo (asst. trainer), Addie Tambellini, Norm Lenardon, Gerry Penner, Seth Martin, Hugh McIntyre, Laurie Bursaw, Bobby Kromm (coach).
Missing - Jackie McLeod, Claude Cyr, Mike Legace

HENRY NEWTON SMITH

If you're from the Town of Trail and you're not Italian male,

The challenge is a little bit too much.

It would be fairly easy if you were from Brindisi,

Or if you had that polished Roman touch.

But if you're Irish-British and just a little skittish,

You're forced to prove yourself a better man.

It is therefore even rougher when expected to be tougher,

Your answer to each challenge is, "I can,"

For someone who is cocky, the future lies in hockey

Where you must shine as tough guy on the team.

The World Cup made us famous, the Smokeaters they named us

And in the hockey world we were supreme.

When you've scaled those lofty heights it's not hard to set your sights

On being successful in the business world.

For over fifty years with blood and sweat and tears

The flags of some great businesses unfurled,

Each business one and all would start off rather small

And soon there would be talk of it expanding.

Using all his hockey skills Harry Smith enjoyed the thrills

Of each and every contract he was landing.

Some hotels in Castlegar where his brother tended bar

Were just the start of something really big.

With oil and gas and lubes and Esso grease in tubes

While H.N. got the most from every rig.

Continued………

Continued………

So then he felt desire to sell it all, retire,

Vancouver Island was his lucky choice.

He could not change his ways, it only took five days

And folks around Victoria heard that voice.

To no one's real surprise he turned his business eyes,

To see if he could organize and buy,

An agency or two, or something else to do,

As usual the limit was the sky.

He just could do no wrong so it did not take long

To build the biggest outfit selling oil.

With diesel fuel and gas, Cardlocks of Island Pass,

Son Jim and Bruce continue there to toil.

So then he gets a taste of business handling waste

It's pumping out, instead of filling tanks.

He's often heard to mutter, "your waste's my bread and butter"

And now his septic outfit really cranks.

With someone who's this bright, who works hard day and night

There comes a time when he should take a rest.

In spite of this I'm glad, to say that this young lad

Feels that the years ahead will be the best.

Just three score years and ten, he'll likely start again

There's time for him to make another hit.

So stand and raise your glass, let not this moment pass

And join me in a toast to Harry Smith.

I WONDER

Please think about it, if you can
And tell me how it all began.
I'd also really like to know,
Just how far back we'd have to go.
I think we'll need a crystal ball
To find out just who caused it all.
Let's face it, we are in the dark
About who taught a dog to bark.
And have you heard a cat meow,
Or listened to a mooing cow.
And how about a horse's neigh
Or growling grizzly bears at play.
And then there is the eagle's screech
Or squawking herons on the beach.
There's many more surprising things,
How does an egg develop wings?
And have you seen the salmon spawn
Or checked the ant hills in your lawn?
A caterpillar crawling by
Will soon become a butterfly
A bumble bee will fly around,
How does it make that buzzing sound?
And then the greatest show on earth
The magic of a baby's birth.
So every day I look about,
I'm more convinced and have no doubt,
That there's a God not far away,
Directing us from day to day.

IF ONLY

There is a phrase that I hear much too often,

And my reaction to it does not soften.

Most people use it as a kind of crutch,

Which indicates that they're not thinking much.

It's often used when things do not go well

And there is no excuse for them to tell.

So that if things go wrong or even bad

You will hear the phrase "if only I had".

"If only", "if only", or maybe, "I wish"

Which causes me anger and some anguish.

When things do not go the way that you want

The worst thing to do is to let it taunt

Your mind, so that you can't think clearly.

A circumstance which could cost you dearly.

Much better to rid yourself of this phrase

And have no regrets the rest of your days.

My mother was a born optimist, as was her father before her. I never heard either my parents or my grandad say "if only". They accepted people at their face value. They had no time for negative feelings and were well-liked and respected. I never heard either of my folks criticize anyone, or complain. They lived for each day and each other. Live and let live.

BILL MOORE
OF
WINTER HARBOUR

IN THE PINK (CORAL, THAT IS!)

In the year of our Lord, nineteen twenty-two,
A boy-child was born, near the Stanley Park Zoo.
His father was happy, his mother was glad
When they looked at the size of this fine Irish lad.
"He'll make a great logger," his dad said with pride,
As he looked at the baby, being held by his bride.
"He's strong in the back, has the arms of a champ,
Some day he may own, his own logging camp."

They left the big city, to head up the Coast
With a fine healthy son, and a reason to boast.
The ship headed out, for a logging camp bound,
To a place near Cape Scott, called Quatsino Sound.
The work there was hard, and conditions were rough,
You couldn't survive there, unless you were tough.
Well the baby matured, as a hard working boy,
To his friends he was faithful, to his parents a joy.

When his father passed on, to that camp in the sky,
There was no time to mourn, even less time to cry,
At age twenty-one, he faced up to his loss,
And took on the title, of logging camp "boss".
This meant working hard, to get logs in the chuck,
With skill, luck and courage, made many a buck.
His crusty old crew, just did what they did,
With the greatest respect for this gutsy young kid.

Continued………

Continued.........

There were hard times, misfortunes, the odd tidal wave,
But in spite of adversity, he never gave
An inch, or a fraction, or thought he might quit,
This man was as hard, as a rock driller's bit.
Even now after years, in the North Island bush,
He merits respect as the best kind of "push",
To make a success, of each tough logging show,
And keep the respect, of all those in the know.

To the North and the South, to the East and the West,
It's widely agreed, that his crew is the best,
He works along with them, while logging each "side",
By his own good example, develops their pride.
His camp is a model, of what camps should be
Surrounded by woods at the edge of the sea,
His equipment is well-kept, all paid for we think,
Not painted in yellow, it's all coral pink.

Which makes one realize, that this man has a heart,
Expressing himself through industrial art.
His musical choices are jazzy and wide,
Jazz fests at the Harbour, are held there with pride.
So now as I bring my short poem to its end,
I'm proud I can call this great man my good friend.
He's welcomed us all, as a most gracious host,
So pick up your glass, and we'll all drink a toast.

To Bill Moore!
One of my best friends owned and operated a logging camp in "Downtown" Winter Harbour. He was a down-to-earth logger who was comfortable in any company. He had many interests and served on the National Safety Council, was President of the Truck Logger's Association and President of the Pacific Logging Congress among many other activities such as a founding Director of the Mount Waddington Regional District. A keen jazz fan, he ran Jazz Festivals at Winter Harbour which attracted many famous musicians over the years.

His eldest son, Dr. Patrick Moore, a scientist, was one of the founders of Greenpeace and a sensible voice for practical rational environmentalism like his logger father.

The "pink" in the title of this poem refers to the coral-pink used to brighten the logging trucks and heavy logging and road-building equipment at Winter Harbour.

IN VINO VERITAS?

A menu describing good wine

Is really not hard to define.

The tendency is to use words

That are much in vogue in the 'burbs,

"Soft-textured", "full-bodied" and "firm",

So "zingy" and "tasty", each term

Designed to intrigue and incite

Desire to please your appetite.

The reader just cannot resist

Those well-chosen words with a twist.

"Approachable", "brooding" and "keen",

All words from the wine-tasting scene.

"Buttery", "deep" and "refreshing",

Roll off the tongue like a blessing.

These words make me ponder and think,

We're only describing a drink,

So "dark" and so "deep" and so "clear",

The same could be said about beer.

Dedicated to the menu writers who write the menus for British Airways and dedicated to my friend Merv Isert, the only oenologist that I know.

INDEFINABLE

We think that we can define time

And distance by measurement.

We use words like second, minute,

Hour, day, week, month or year.

And recently, the word century was in vogue.

But these words define only portions of time.

There is no beginning to time

And, apparently, no ending....

It is a bit like distance.

We have our words to describe portions of distance.

Inch, foot, yard, mile, kilometer,

Based on the arm or leg of some King,

A long time ago.

More recently, some genius measured the distance

From the North Pole to the Equator,

Which itself was equidistant.

From each pole,

And broke it down into kilometers

And meters.

Continued.........

Continued………

If the Polar ice caps melt

Will a meter shrink?

And, as with time

Distance has no start, no finish,

No beginning and no end.

Scary.

Paint a line to the furthest star.

Then keep painting in the same direction,

To the next distant star that you can see.

Repeat this in any direction.

From any point on earth.

North, South, East or West.

None of those lines will reach the edge.

Those lines go on forever.

They have no end.

Neither does the time it takes.

Both indefinable.

To those who have stared out at a night sky and wondered where the "edge" is, and how long it would take to get there.

IN THE LAND OF THE BLIND, THE ONE EYED MAN IS KING

I think of the people around me
And think of the people I've met,
I think of how much they confound me
And how they have got what they get.

There are quite a few folks among them,
Who owe their success to hard work
And some opportunities flung them,
Who could see the light through the murk.

There's some who had education,
Did well in school and in college,
Then built a good reputation,
Based on a surplus of knowledge.

Some others were born into money,
A big silver spoon in their mouth.
They holiday where it is sunny
And if things go wrong they just pout.

Then there are those that amaze me,
They look like they've just won it all,
So much like my mentor before me,
Who said "keep your eye on the ball."

My mentor was one of the men
Who had what it took to succeed
He taught me the power of the pen
And not to be frightened to lead.

"IRELAND" THE FIRST COLONY OF THE BRITISH EMPIRE

To begin with
There never was a border between North and South,
After all, they lived on an island,
They had their battles,
But for thousands of years
They shared that island,
A past and a future.
They became the very first colony
Of the British Empire,
Against their wishes.
After eight hundred years of occupation
The colonizers withdrew to a quarter of the island,
In the North-East corner.
A man-made border was laid out
By a British army officer named Bourdillon,
The Boundary Commissioner,
Who left, for his own safety, for Canada,
With his family in 1922.
The border and the ideas behind it,
Have worn out.
The concrete blockades and the razor-wire are gone.
The border no longer exists
And there are a lot of unemployed border guards,
The way that it should be,
And the anti-British murals in the Falls Road
Have become a tourist attraction,
The way that it should be...........

Having cycled and hitch-hiked around Northern Ireland when it was a "troubled" state, I was pleased to drive around there recently and find it as peaceful as any other part of the country. The border has disappeared and the people of North and South are living peacefully together. It will take a few years to forget the "Troubles" and the extreme antagonism that existed there for so many years, but the Irish are an optimistic lot. This poem was written in Belfast.

IRELAND'S LOSS, CANADA'S GAIN

A land where agriculture held the sway,
Where landlords, absentee, lived far away,
Whose Agents served their masters very well
And put their tenants through a kind of hell,
Who worked so hard on every day they could
To earn enough to keep themselves in food.
These people struggled hard from day to day,
In front of them a life of hardship lay,

While riches filled the pockets of the few,
For them there was naught else that they could do.
The chances for success were not so great
The only option was to emigrate.
So, many left their family, friends and home,
Adventure bound, they were inclined to roam.
They traveled to the North and to the West
And settled where they thought they could do best.

Some others traveled South and to the East,
To Africa, not scared by man or beast.
They fought in many wars and many lands
Through jungle, bush and veldt and desert sands,
Faced challenges and every kind of strife
The only way to find a better life.
To Canada these people were a gift.
Their efforts gave the country such a lift

Continued.........

Continued.........

Through the years the flow of emigrants grew

Not just from Ireland, other countries too.

They brought with them a willingness to work

Put in long hours, from danger did not shirk.

They gambled in the long run that they'd win

Though pay for lowly jobs was very thin.

They took the jobs that no one else would take

But had to start somewhere to make their stake.

They helped to build the railways and the roads,

Developed farms and soon produced train loads

Of agriculture products that soon rolled

To ports on East and West coast to be sold.

Some others worked in mines or in the woods,

Producing different ores and lumber goods.

Though it is sad they had to emigrate,

Their impact on this country has been great.

*Written to honour the many emigrants with whom I have worked in business and in politics.
They have made a huge contribution to Canada in a relatively short period of time.*

IRISH BLESSINGS

If the problems of life get too pressing,

You can always come up with a blessing.

People who come from the Emerald Isle,

Have blessings galore to fit any style.

"May a strong wind always be at your back."

"A bushel of luck, may you never lack."

"When it is cold, may you have a warm breeze."

"Enjoy every day, with ease as you please."

"The worst day of your future far exceed,

The very best day of your past, indeed."

"On a dark night, may you have a full moon."

"Enjoy this life's race, don't finish too soon."

"May those who love us, keep their feelings strong,

And if they do not, God show them they're wrong.

But if they won't change, may such worthless wimp,

Break both his legs, and be known by his limp."

IT'S A KILLER BUT NOT A WHALE

We know this is the very wild West Coast,
About which we don't hesitate to boast.
It's shores are lined with trees of evergreen,
The greatest forests that have ever been.
While mountains, river valleys, frame the view,
Its beauties bound to leave a breathless you.
These rivers breeding grounds for our wild fish,
The answer to each sportsman's every wish.
The fish in turn provide a great food source,
For seals, sea lions and dolphins, the main course.
Best known of the lot, the Orca Killer,
To whale watch folks, the industry's pillar.
The truth, of course, is that it's wrong to call,
A "killer whale" is not a whale at all.

An Orca scientist will be heard to rail,
Should he or she hear you call it a whale.
The fact is that it's of the dolphin kind,
It's trying to leave a nasty name behind.
`Twould please me greatly if by voice or pen,
I do not have to hear that name again.
The animal itself is quite a sight,
In shiny black and patches of pure white.
"Whale" watch season is now getting longer,
Interest in the beast is getting stronger.
Folks kayak, sail, or go by motor boat
And find that Orca groups are nothing loathe,
To jump and swim and dive, display their skills,
Their actions all provide such wondrous thrills.

*Dedicated to the folks who have pioneered whale-watching expeditions from various ports
on Vancouver Island but especially to those who started it all at Telegraph Cove.*

LEAVING HOME

With sadness in my heart,
I made the move to part,
The country of my birth and of my dreams.
I headed far away,
To where I live today,
`Twas only yesterday, or so it seems.
I saw so many places,
All kinds of different faces,
In lands untamed and best described as wild.
I headed `way out West,
It seemed to be the best,
The beauty of its Coast had me beguiled.
I landed in B.C.
The greatest place to be,
And looked around to see what I could do.
I figured that I could,
Get work at logging wood,
The challenge was to find a logging crew.
In old Vancouver town,
Were loggers of renown,
Who hired out when they'd spent their hard-earned stake.
I hung around with some,
Like any other bum,
And found out just what it would really take.
I bought a Stanfield shirt,
Which did not show the dirt,
A pair of Pierre Paris spiked caulk boots.
I packed them in my grip
And went to board the ship,
Surrounded by some tough and scary brutes.

Continued………

Continued………

I landed in the camp,

Another choker champ

Intent on being the very best I could.

I'd do my level best,

To pass the logger's test,

There never was a doubt. I knew I would.

I liked the time spent there

And all that great fresh air,

`Twas everything that I had dreamed about.

I had the greatest hopes

And quickly learnt the ropes,

As well as any other logging lout.

And each day out at work

I learnt you cannot shirk,

Accept the fact that you must pull your weight.

The others on our crew

All knew just what to do,

Their reputation was indeed first rate.

I never had a doubt

That things would all work out,

The company made profit and no loss,

I worked hard through the years

And overcame my fears

And soon I was promoted to be boss.

Dedicated to the following group of Managers who over the years, managed the Port McNeill operations of the Alaska Pine and Cellulose Company, Rayonier Canada (BC) Ltd., Western Forest Products under their long-term nickname "Pioneer Timber":

Don Beise, Keith Beise, Trevor Boniface, Mickey Brown, Archie Byers, Dale Chilton, Al Clarke, Bernie Clarke, Lloyd Ekholm, Gary Griffith, Archie Hallberg, Bob Halgren, Harvey Hurd, Roger Manning, Fred Mantic, Ian Paterson, Bert Peck, Pat Schreiber, Vern Roberts, Carl Yzerman and Bernie Zimmerman most of whom started their forestry careers setting chokers.

LIFE'S UPS AND DOWNS OR GENTLEMEN BE SEATED

In modern times there are many rhymes

That suit our human quirks,

But none that beat the toilet seat

And how it really works.

For man and boy, let's not be coy,

There are times they use the seat.

Maybe once a day they go that way,

It keeps the bathroom neat.

And ladies all, both short and tall

Will sit each time they go

If the seat's not down, they'll always frown

And moan about their beau.

They'll say that lout, should think about

Us ladies who must sit,

We hope that soon, he'll change his tune

And stop being such a twit.

Continued………

Continued........

But he in turn, will start to burn

If the seat is not left up

When in a rush, to kidney flush

Having had too much to sup,

So you can see, with he and she

A point they each have got.

But as a rule, you'd be a fool

Between them to get caught.

It makes good sense to avoid offence

And reach a compromise

So they must try, both gal and guy

To act in a way that's wise,

If he is kind to her behind

He'll bend and downward shift it

And she in turn, won't make him burn

By forcing him to lift it.

In the never-ending argument of the toilet seat wars, there is but one fair solution. This indisputably,
is *the best cure for the ups and downs of the toilet seats everywhere. He leaves it down and she*
leaves it up.

LIMERICKS AND SUNDRIES

TO THE BELLY DANCERS

They danced from the right and the left
With steps that were classy and deft.
They jiggled their bellies
Like so many jellies,
We came, we saw and we wept.

TO A GUITAR PLAYER

My good friend old Craig's never wrong
Although in the tooth he is long,
While strumming his thing
He broke his G-string
And now he can't sing us a thong.

SMILE

To the most beautiful girl in the world
Whose hair is never curled,
Whose sloppy walk and crazy smile
Would make a nutcase walk a mile.
This poem is writ with you in mind
I like your crazy walk and smile
It makes me want to run a mile.

BIG MAC

A young man that I know as Jack
Was seen walking home with a sack
Full of goodies so neat
From MacDonalds to treat
The approach of a Big Mac attack.

WALT

There was a young fellow named Walt
In love with his poems' gestalt,
He scribbles away, on a poem a day,
I do think he is worth his salt.

LOST

She was a folk singer

A musician working hard

To please the crowd

With her mandolin, her guitar

And her violin.

She was hesitant in her singing

A faint voice, an uncertain tone.

She was a groupie

And a member of a trio

That sang and played together well.

They each chose a solo,

Their favourite song,

Unaccompanied, a capella.

Her's was about her trip to India

Where she went to find herself

And never did.

Maybe, just maybe

She was looking in the wrong place

She still looks lost,

Though a mirror might help.

Written during a musical performance by three travelling musicians/singers. One of them talked about going to India "to find herself". She was a talented musician and could have saved herself the trip to India, if she took a good look at herself in a mirror.

A chokerman "pulling rigging"

89

MEMORIES, GETTING SENTIMENTAL

We've worked away for many, many years

And given our share of blood and sweat and tears.

It hasn't been a very easy ride,

With few who were prepared to take our side.

We've dealt with heavy weather, rain and storm,

Such tough conditions are the daily norm.

In summer there's a chance of forest fire,

Because the heat makes forests so much drier.

Believe me when I say it's not a gift

When we are called to work on early shift.

In wintertime the challenge is the rain,

Takes months before we see much sun again.

And there are days we face the heavy snows,

Most likely when that cold North West wind blows.

But loggers are a brave and happy lot,

Complain about the weather they will not.

When in the woods they stick to a routine,

With each man working like a smooth machine.

They'll spend a day on hillsides cold and damp

And cheerfully at night head back to camp.

Where each has got his own and lonely bunk,

A locker and a shelf to store his junk.

And in the cookhouse where they go to eat,

Each logger has his designated seat.

They work hard and they're proud of what they do.

Their workplace oft described as just a zoo.

Continued………

Continued.........

The names they used developed over time,

Butt-rigging, main-line, haul-backs and strawline.

With hookers, side-rods and a whistle punk,

They had some crazy names for all their junk.

With cats and donkey engines all around.

A line horse and a rig-up goat are found,

A bull-pin's fitted on each logging truck,

A bull-pen in the boom down at the chuck.

A safety lever which is called a "dog",

Will hold a gear when it falls in a cog.

There's a bull-block at the top of every spar

And bulldozers can be found, near and far.

Cat skinners, shovel-runners, drillers too,

Are all familiar members of the crew.

In honour of some Irish logger's wife

They'll trust a Molly Hogan with their life.

The blasters known as powder-monkeys, rue

The day they became members of this zoo.

With chasers, loaders, riggers, chokermen,

Oh, wouldn't it be great to start again?

The unusual names used to describe logger and logging equipment intrigued me when I first experienced logging-camp life. Living in bunkhouses exposed us to great stories and some very interesting people who took the isolation, the extremes of weather and the privation, in their stride. Loggers were and are exceptional people. They don't shirk from work, danger, isolation or tough conditions. This one's for them.

MERRY WIDOW MOUNTAIN

On Merry Widow Mountain was a Mine,
That produced iron-ore for quite a time.
The ore was dug from deep within a pit,
High quality, with customers a hit.
Two hundred miners worked there night and day,
Did all within their power to make 'er pay.
A fleet of belly-dump-trucks hauled the ore,
At fifty tons a load and sometimes more.
The trucks ran day and night throughout the week,
A narrow gravel road, not for the meek.
A fifty mile round trip for every load,
'Twas hard to keep eighteen wheels on the road.
Mechanics kept the trucks in running shape,
Most of whom had a penchant for the grape.
They worked hard and they put in lengthy hours,
With no time off, a bunkhouse life soon sours.
So after months of working every day,
They'd quit the job and take a holiday.
The length of holiday that they would take,
Relied upon the dollars in their stake.
Depending on the pleasures they might seek,
Some would be back in Camp within a week.
In days the total savings would be spent
On taxes, meals and booze and girlfriend's rent.
And then 'twas time to make a sad phone call
To our old friend down at the Hiring Hall.

Dedicated to the hard-rock miners who pioneered the Mining Industry along the B.C. Coast, especially to the open-pit iron miners on Merry Widow Mountain, 25 miles south of Port McNeill in the winter of 1956.

MORNING COFFEETIME

The only way to start the day

Is at my neighbourhood café.

The coffee brewing in its pot,

Served by the mug-full, piping hot.

I watch the townsfolk waking up,

As on their mugs they sip and sup.

The rains may fall, the winds may blow,

There may be ice, there may be snow.

But when you're sitting warm and smug,

Enjoying that morning coffee mug,

There's nothing that can get you down

In this North Island logging town.

There are a few great people-watching and listening places in Port McNeill, where you can enjoy your morning coffee and hear some great logging, mining and fishing stories.

MV CAPE BEALE

There is a fine old ship that sails the Coast.
A ship of which her owner loves to boast.
As the power of diesel fuel drives her along,
Her rigging hums a very happy song.
The skipper standing tall behind the wheel
Is just the kind of man who makes you feel
That while he's on the bridge and in command
He's steering with a firm and steady hand.
Both ship and skipper have that salty look
Of subjects from an old adventure book.
She started out in life to harvest fish
And lived up to her owner's every wish
Her crew all sang her praises long and loud
Being on a top producer made them proud,
The fastest boat among the fishing fleet
Her catch would always top the high-catch sheet.
But then the years of work began to show
Compared to newer boats she was too slow.
Her owner said it's time for rest and leisure
And transformed her to a ship for family pleasure.
She meets her happy owner's fondest wish
As now she catches sun instead of fish
And as the owner changed his good ship's role
He analyzed himself and searched his soul
In politics 'til then he'd spent his life
And now the time had come to leave the strife
So in an effort to make life much brighter
He's now become quite famous as a writer.
And proves that with his skill and written word
That yes, the pen is mightier than the sword.

This beautiful pleasure boat was once a high-producing seine boat. It was converted by Gordon Gibson Senior, who was an outspoken politician and a successful forest company owner. He was famously known as The Bull of the Woods when he pioneered a new way of logging and transporting logs safely from the Queen Charlotte Islands to the mills in the Vancouver area. His son, Gordon, now skippers the vessel on jaunts to various places up and down the West Coast

NATIONAL EMBLEMS

The Shamrock, the Thistle, the Leek and the Rose,
Are symbols of nations that everyone knows.
Now each of these nations developed their styles
Well known 'round the world as the famed British Isles.
The Rose is best known as a symbol of beauty,
Its people best known for adherence to duty.
In all parts of England this lovely flower grows
And nothing compares to a fine English Rose.
The Welsh people use as their symbol the Leek,
A nation of people not known to be weak.
They stay to themselves in a land that is great.
Well known for their singing, they don't emigrate.
Scotsmen decided to honour the Thistle.
Don't call them Scotchmen, they're likely to bristle.
Their men walk around in these bright tartan shirts
And will not admit what they wear 'neath their skirts.
Which brings us around to the lovely Shamrock,
The Irish who love to sing, laugh, joke and talk.
They've helped to pioneer the wild lands of the North,
Where living conditions are well-known to sort
Out the strong from the weak, and those who will stay
And give a real decent day's work for their pay.
They've settled in cities, in big and small towns
And learnt to survive in political bounds.
They tend to be faithful when they take your side,
Adopt their new country with well-founded pride.
Now English and Scotsmen and Welshmen please note,
These verses were penned by a fine Irish poet.
So if you want more about you to be writ,
You'll have to go find your own Doctor of Lit.
And if on the meaning of Lit. you're not sure,
It"s just a short way to spell out Literature.

Many of the original settlers in Canada, came from the British Isles. In many cases they were leaving tough and poor circumstances and taking a huge gamble in emigrating. They each brought their own way of contributing to their new home.

NO LIMITS, NO BEGINNING, NO END

There is nothing as indefinable

As time or distance.

How far does distance stretch?

How long does time go?

No matter where we look

Distance stretches in front of us

For all time.

Choose any direction

Go to the furthest star you can see,

North, South, East or West

Or even in between.

When you get there, rest.

Now look ahead in the same direction,

Just more distance

There is no edge, no end,

In any direction.

Time is as indefinable,

But can only be measured in two ways,

Forward and backwards.

When did time start,

When does it finish,

Did it ever have a start,

Will it ever have a finish,

Has anyone set the alarm,

Does anyone care?

NO ONE WILL CARE

Sometimes there's a reason for us to be mad,

Sometimes we weaken and it makes us sad.

It may happen once, should not happen twice,

Losing your temper is not very nice.

So please mark my words when you hear me say.

`Twill be forgotten a year from today.

There will be odd times as you live your life.

You will be tested with pressure and strife.

You may be too young or maybe too old,

To accept advice when you are being told.

Again mark my words when you hear me say.

`Twill be all the same a year from today.

And sure as there is a moon up above,

There will be times when you think you're in love.

You may be asked for a kiss or a hug,

Please don't refuse it by acting too smug.

Once more mark my words, the third time I say,

There's no one will care a year from today.

So don't spare your kisses, pass them around,

There is much pleasure in them to be found.

You'll never know what you've lost or you'll miss,

By not saying "yes" when offered a kiss.

In a love story you give and you get,

Make a decision you will not regret.

So please hear me well, once more when I say,

There's no one will care, a year from today.

NO SLEEP

I know I'm not the greatest poet

Believe me, when I say I know it.

But I enjoy spending the time

To think of all the words that rhyme.

That help me to explain my view

To all my friends, including you.

When day is done, I go to bed,

A myriad thoughts swirl through my head,

And when those thoughts get 'way too deep

I find it hard to get to sleep.

So here I am, at dead of night,

Just wide awake needing to write.

To sort these thoughts out, heap by heap,

As otherwise I'll get no sleep.

ODE TO A GUINNESS

Joyous nectar, golden brown
A hint of gold with pearly crown
Tasteful strong yet soft and mellow
To win the heart of any fellow.
And if it's fellow winning lass
Then offer her a brimful glass,
To complement her many charms.

And she will end up in your arms.

LET'S HAVE ANOTHER!

Ah, the joy of it,
A strong thirst to satisfy,
After the game, companionship,
The need to quench,
Only one answer,
Michael, a round please
Of your best, what else man?
Guinness of course.
Dark brown nectar
Riffles of gold
That creamy crown,
For this wondrous gift
The Lord be truly thanked.

A few years ago the Guinness Company held a competition for advertising ideas. These were my entries. They didn't win, but it was fun to enter.

ODE TO A SPEED DEMON

The Mountie sat in his little black car

Driving along with the window ajar,

The night was warm and the weather was dry

The moon shone down from a cloudless sky,

When out of the dark and dreary night

There came a flashing hurtling light,

The Mountie looked up with consternation

And said 'tis a UFO attack on the nation,

But he looked again as the light got bigger

And saw what looked like a human figure,

Crouched up and clutching the steering wheel

In a death-defying grip of steel,

'Twas a Detroit monster built for speed

With the strength of the thousand horse-power breed,

It passed down the road in a cloud of dust

Satisfying the driver's speed-starved lust,

With the throttle pressed tightly into the floor

Hurtling along at ninety or more,

The Mountie turned 'round his trusty steed

And drove in pursuit at increasing speed,

The needle crept up to ninety-five

Controlled by the fastest Mountie alive.

Continued.........

Continued.........

He winced but he firmly set his jaw

He knew he was breaking the traffic-speed law,

Doing ninety-five in a thirty-mile zone

He was glad in a way he was all alone,

As the needle crept up to a hundred and ten

He changed into third and pressed throttle again,

He was catching up fast now and flashing his light

When the driver in front turned around and went white,

He pulled to the side and the Mountie shot past

He couldn't slow down he was travellin' so fast,

But finally braked and slid to a halt

Skid-marking the pavement but 'twasn't his fault,

He jumped from his car as the speeder pulled in

The squeal of his brakes stirring up quite a din,

And there on his face was an angelic smile

There's no doubt said the Mountie, this chap's got style,

Out came the notebook and down went the facts

The speeder was jail-bound because of his acts,

The judge passing sentence said "what's your excuse"

The speeder just smiled and said "please turn me loose",

"Like our great Highway's Minister, I hate standing still,

If Gaglardi can do it, then so can Flying Bill".........

A young man from England, living in Campbell River, showed a great interest in the North Island and its potential. He visited us often. He liked to drive very fast and compare himself to the then Minister of Highways," Flying" Phil Gaglardi. The Mountie who stopped him for breaking the speed-limit was not very sympathetic to his excuse for speeding.

This is dedicated to Bill Macadam.

OH OH SEVEN EVENT AT OH OH SEVEN HILLS

Our plan is that we WILL promote

This little piece of heaven,

And to this end we'll utilize

The theme of Oh Oh Seven,

On April twenty one we'll meet

At Golf Club Seven Hills,

To analyze the challenges

Of our economic ills.

We trust the folks attending

Will arrive with open minds,

And actively participate,

Not just sit on their behinds.

Our regional economic development commission organized a promotional symposium for elected and appointed officials at the regional golf course called Seven Hills. I wrote this poem as a reminder to the participants to be open-minded and participate actively.

OH! DEER

Our lovely land of mountains, lakes and trees,
Has many features that will surely please,
Our visitors and residents alike
When traveling by car, by boat or bike.
And when we're in the hinterland or wilds,
Raw nature is all 'round us and beguiles.
Well noted for its beauty and its game,
These animals are wild and rarely tame.
The cougar is the wildest of the lot,
A friendly type of animal, it's not.
And then we have two different kinds of bear
And each of them should be approached with care.
The grizzly bear, most dangerous of all,
Most likely to attack and kill or maul.
The black bear is as wild but somewhat kinder,
Be careful if her cubs are close behind her.
We've also got big elk and even moose,
With little human contact, they hang loose.
Surprisingly, most dangerous of all
In Winter, Spring or Summer and in Fall
The Bambi deer, its mother and its dad,
For killing people they are really bad.
They've killed more people than have all the rest.
Most dangerous animal across the West.
They like to graze beside a traveled road
And jump in front of traffic, every mode.
They're really very fast upon their feet
And sometimes think that they can even beat
A vehicle too late for it to yield
And end up crashing through the glass windshield.

Slow down, it could save your life.

OH, BRANDY

Brandy!
The word rolled off his lips
Delicately, sensitively,
As if he was tasting his dream,
A connoisseur of pronunciation, articulation,
And, Brandy.
He was bearded, grayish, wore glasses,
And was twice her age.
Old enough to know better,
A dreamer, and a boy again at heart,
Smitten by her beauty, her youth
And her name.....
Intoxicated by that name.
He was explaining, with great authority
And firm conviction
Some technical detail
On a land-use planning map
As only a true bureaucrat can.
She epitomized, in a transcendental way
The expectations of her name.
She pretended interest, as if she understood.
She didn't, and she didn't care.
With her looks and a name like that,
She didn't have to,
Oh, Brandy.

At a meeting of the Land and Resources Management Committee in Nanaimo, I overheard a civil servant explaining details on some maps which were on display in the foyer of the meeting place hotel. This poem describes the scene and Brandy's feigned interest.

ONE MAN'S REFLECTION

There's a person on whom every man must depend,

A person that should be a very good friend,

On whom we should place our most personal trust,

There are times in our lives when we must.

There are times when he keeps us under control

When faced with our foibles, a most worthy goal.

He lives through our sadness and savours our joys

And helps us to meet each challenge with poise.

And once in a while when we're tempted to stray

As we struggle along in life, day to day.

We test his resolve to the end of his limit

So it's good that he has so much strength to put in it.

We owe him our thanks and our deep gratitude

For helping to cheer us when in a sad mood.

Whenever our ego is bursting with pride

And we need a reminder and someone to chide

Us, he is sure to be there with a hint that our goal

Is to live every day with some basic control.

Continued………

And if we tell lies, take no care with the truth

We're sure to receive an imaginary boot

To remind us that honour requires us to tell

The truth at all times, or our life will be hell.

Which brings us around to the truth of this tale

Just who is this helpful mysterious male.

Who enables each man through life safely to pass

He's the man that we see every day in the glass.

The man in the mirror we see every morning

Has a look in his eye we should take as a warning.

He can be a good friend or a very bad foe

So it's all up to you, as to which way you go.

Look him straight in the eye every morning and night

And he'll help you decide what's wrong and what's right.

ONE WAY TO SPEND THE WINTER

When we were logging we thought we were tough,

We worked 'longside the toughest of the tough,

At times we did not think that we'd survive,

Surprised ourselves by somehow staying alive.

Then Winter came and camps were all shut down.

Our logging buddies headed off for town,

To spend their money on a winter fling

And live the city life until the Spring.

They'd party 'til they'd spent their hard-earned poke

And head for camp again when they were broke.

Of all the people on our logging crew

My pal and I decided that we two

Would skip the holidays and spend our time

In helping build road access to a mine.

Construction people were a crazy lot,

Like civilized tough loggers they were not.

Their project was to build a mine-haul road

Across which streams of mud and water flowed.

They lived in a rough bunkhouse-camp on wheels,

A cook called Jimmy Campbell made the meals.

A diesel generator supplied lights

And heat and comfort through those wintry nights.

We worked long hours there each and every day,

Determined that we'd really make it pay.

Continued………

Continued.........

The loggers had built road to mile fourteen,

Through pristine forests few had ever seen.

A valley stretched ahead with many lakes

And our construction crew had what it takes

To get ten miles of road built to the mine,

With some delays brought on by Christmas-time.

When half the crew got homesick and went home,

A haywire crew was left there all alone.

On Christmas Eve the freight-truck brought good news,

Ten mail bags full of mail and lots of booze.

Instead of spending Christmas kinda dry,

Most of the crew spent Christmas rather high.

The kitchen crew joined in the festive mood

They cooked up every kind of Christmas food.

On Boxing Day we all got back to work,

This was a crew that never thought to shirk.

That one day off was such a welcome break,

But it was all the time the crew would take.

We worked away and gave the job our all,

Until the joy of work began to pall.

And when the rain turned into heavy snow,

We headed for the sun in Mexico.

When logging shut down in October 1956, my pal and I went to work with a Construction crew that were building ten miles of road to Merry Widow Mountain near Benson Lake. We lived in two primitive construction camps, one near Three Isle Lake and one near the top of Maynard Lake at the Raging River Bridge. There was no comparison between life in those camps and the civilized crew in our logging camp. It was very different.

OTTAWA PATRONAGE, BY GUM!

When Dave lost his job as MP,

Jean Chretien said, "now let me see,

To save him being skint,

He could run the Mint,

'Tis just the right job for Dave D."

But being so close to that cash,

Made Dave just a little bit rash.

He acted quite silly,

Spent cash willy nilly

And went on a wild spending bash.

His spending-spree gave us a hint,

How taxpayers' money is spent.

Dave D. was so dumb,

He expensed his chewing gum

I just hope the chewing gum was Mint.

One of Prime Minister Chretien's Cabinet Ministers, David Dingwall, lost his seat in an election and was appointed by the Prime Minister to manage the Canadian Mint. His expenses at the Mint were questioned by the press and an expenditure of $1.35 for a pack of chewing gum, was noted in a press story. I wondered if his favourite flavour was MINT.

PLAN AHEAD!

A challenge in life is dealing with strife
And getting the best from each day.
But if you're in doubt, one needs to look out
And hopefully find a new way.

You must plan ahead, it's so easily said,
Because every deep thinking man
Has got to give thought and do what he ought
To be just the best that he can.

But there is a chance that trying to advance
He's likely to take the wrong tack
And that's a mistake, so easy to make
You can't move ahead looking back.

You should not waste time in trying to define
Whatever tomorrow may bring,
Avoid all the stress, just think of success
That hard-to-find illusive thing.

So plan well today and heed what I say
Today's the best day of them all
You're bound to succeed, so listen and heed
Then this simple message recall.

You must keep in mind, that looking behind
Will really not help going ahead
Just forget the past, keep travelling fast
You're bound to come out way ahead.

PRINCESSES AT THE TEMPLE OF ICE

'Tis early morning
The stands at the Arena,
This glorious well-lit Temple of Ice,
Are full of anxious faces.
Patient faces of grandparents,
Young, fresh faces
Of the sisters, brothers and pals,
And the hopeful faces
Of the moms and dads
Will she win? Will she fall?
How do the judges decide?
They sit on a platform
At center ice, serious,
Their backs to us,
As we ponder and hope.
How can they tell who is best,
When each of these kids is so good?
The would-be stars
Gather at the entrance gate,
Pacing back and forth on their skate protectors,
We, too, are their protectors.
With their fancy outfits, hair-dos and make up,
Chosen carefully to suit their music
And the judges.
The music starts, the tests begin
And we cheer on our heroines,
Trying to control our emotions
And the butterflies in our bellies.

The seriousness of figure skating came home to me when my wife and I drove 150 miles to the ice arena in Courtenay to watch our granddaughter and her best pals compete in figure-skating tests. The kids were each given a few minutes to warm up and then each went through her routine for three minutes. They were graded by a panel of judges who have the most difficult job imaginable. To me, all the kids were great as they went through their routine. Surrounded by other grandparents, parents, aunts, uncles and friends, I realized that we, the relatives went through pure suspenseful agony, before, during and after the judging. The kids took it in their stride; I guess that's what it's all about, building character.

PROBLEMS ARISE

When miners open up a mine
There are some things they must define.
Start with a campsite, build a road,
Then tunnel to the motherlode.
It takes good men to do the work,
Avoiding challenges that lurk,
As land is cleared and trees are felled,
With planning meetings daily held.
First build a camp to house the crew,
Create an office, cookhouse too.
Then build a warehouse and a shop
Once it's started, there's no stop,
A light-plant and a first-aid shack,
Of rules and standards there's no lack.
If the campsite's planned with vision,
`Twill contain a sub-division.
Especially in a far off site
To keep a staff that's sharp and bright.
They'll need some kind of shipping port,
To where haul trucks go back and forth.
Supplies of fuel and dynamite,
Go from the port by day and night.
At one mine where I used to work,
The safety rule, they'd often shirk.
And sometimes just to save a buck,
Haul dynamite by gravel truck.
Four hundred cases jammed aboard
A worn-out tandem ten-ton Ford.
And then to keep the cargo dry,
A large tarpaulin they did tie,
With ropes and knots made fast and tight,
No rain could spoil that dynamite.

Continued........

Continued..........

The driver never thought to gripe
At tarp tied 'round the exhaust pipe.
He didn't realize his fix,
When passing fuel truck at mile six.
The fuel truck driver known as "Pop"
Tried everything to make him stop.
But all Pop's efforts were in vain,
The fire got bigger, flame by flame.
Then at the lake up near mile ten,
Old Pop tried passing him again.
He overtook him at high speed
And finally he did succeed.
They tried their best to dump the load,
Right in the middle of the road
But luckily for both of them,
An ore-truck driver known as Ken,
Had stopped and screamed, "For safety sake,
Just drive the truck into the lake."
The burning truck just would not start,
Which almost broke the driver's heart.
The flames had now engulfed each tire,
Which added to the funeral pyre.
Said Ken to Pop, "Drive toward the mine
And I'll stop traffic down the line"
So off they went, one north, one south,
Stopped traffic 'til the fire burnt out.
No traffic moved throughout the night,
In fear of burning dynamite.
And though it made the mine boss curse
There was no doubt, could have been worse.

This poem is written to commemorate a real-life event, where someone made a decision to overload a gravel truck to haul cases of explosives to a mine near Port McNeill. A canvas tarpaulin was tied over the load and made fast to the exhaust pipe. Luckily the dynamite burnt and did not explode.

PROCRASTINATION

My good friend Walt says during May

He'll write a new poem every day.

For me, that is too much, too soon,

I'll try one line a day in June.

And then next month, that is, July,

I'll give two lines a day a try.

Competitions are a bummer,

Not the way to spend a summer.

So maybe I should somehow stall

And not compete with Walt at all.

Once winter winds begin to blow,

He'll lose all interest, that, I know.

Perhaps we should wait until spring,

To start this competition thing?

My poet friend, Walt McConville, likes to test himself, so he wrote to tell me about a challenge he had set for himself. He would write a poem every day for the month of May. Time and my natural limitations, prevented me from accepting the challenge, but I did sit down and reply with a poem of my own in pure self-defence.

QUITE FRANKLY HAS AN EMPTY RING

There are those who speak directly

And get quickly to the point,

There are some who speak correctly

And who do not disappoint.

While others speak more slowly

And who are inclined to natter,

And those who speak so coldly,

But say only things that matter.

As well there are the people

Who just have to be precise.

And some that speak with attitude

That is as warm as ice.

But there are some with minds so numb,

I classify them blankly,

They preface everything they say,

With the silly phrase, "quite frankly".

That phrase is really meaningless

And has an empty ring,

A phrase that is redundant

And does not add a thing.

Frankly - the Oxford Dictionary describes the word as "in a frank manner" or "freely". To me it is as silly as using the word "honestly", or "truthfully". If someone has to tell me they are being "frank", "honest" or "truthful", I wonder why they have to emphasize the fact.

SAM'S SUDS

Some people think that it is fine
To have a daily glass of wine.
There're many others who refrain,
From alcohol that's made from grain.

There are some drinkers 'round about,
That will not touch a drink of stout.
And other rather careful folk,
Who only drink a pop or coke.

There are some people I recall,
Who say it spoils the alcohol,
When any drink you're trying to fix,
Calls for some water or some mix.

The people of teetotal ilk
Will tend to stay with tea or milk.
But mostly all the folks 'round here,
Prefer to have their daily beer.

It helps their mood and appetite
No matter if it's day or night,
In fact it's clear my friends all think,
Beer's much more than a breakfast drink.

One of my best employees and one of my best friends was Sam Schulz who worked with me as a first class driver for many years. Sam looked forward to enjoying a beer on Friday night with two of my other great drivers, Charlie Daly and Ron Lightfoot. Sam would leave the office at the end of the day on Friday with a goodbye and a smile, saying, "time for Sam to have some suds". This is dedicated to the three of them. They were a pleasure to work with and a pleasure to know.

SEASONAL RESPONSE

Psychology of the Gestalt,

Just does not affect my friend Walt.

The poems that he sends me are great,

With help from his sweetheart and mate.

Eileen helps with every confection,

Accepting his kindly direction.

Each poem has a message sincere,

Reflecting the time of the year.

His heartfelt remarks make us proud,

But that, between friends, is allowed.

A poem to my friend, Walt McConville and his wife Eileen

SENATOR BAUCUS AND HIS ATTEMPTS TO FAUCUS!

More hot-air from Senator Baucus

Of the Anti-Canadian caucus,

`twould be nice if ol'Max

Would get off our backs

And be just a little less raucous!

This U.S. Senator from Montana has actively opposed imports of lumber from Canada. His actions belie the intent of the Free Trade Agreement between Canada and the United States.

118

SIDNEY'S POEM FOR DERIAN

I wonder how 'twould feel,

To be a little seal,

And swim around the ocean every day.

I think it would be fine

We'd have a happy time

So I'll jump in with you and we will play.

We will swim with all the fish

If that is what you wish,

And have a feed of shrimp and tasty crab.

We will both be very careful

'Cause my mom is very fearful

In case old shark comes by and makes a grab.

Because to such a fish,

We are just a tasty dish

And he would love to have us in his belly.

So let us never roam

Too far from Nanny's home,

Instead we'll have some cookies watching telly.

This was written with my granddaughter, Sidney Hamilton, when she was six years of age, for her older brother Derian, who was eight at the time, as I was explaining to them how words rhyme. I hope they will enjoy the beauty of poetry as they grow up.

SLICED, COOKED OR RAW

My generation was quite pleased to eat

Good basic meals, potatoes and some meat.

It did not matter if it was just boiled.

Or roasted, fried, minced up, or even broiled.

And if the cooks decided to be nice

They just might add a shake or two of spice.

Perhaps some pepper, thyme or even salt,

Much fancier than that, we'd call a halt.

Then as the means of travel start to change

Our travels take us to some places strange.

We eat Italian food and even French,

Their garlic flavoured snails had quite a stench.

I really liked the food of the Chinese

And also learnt to like Vietnamese.

Japan has got the strangest food I saw,

They like to eat it cold and mostly raw.

Too many choices, don't know what to do,

I think I'd better stay with Irish Stew.

SMILE

If things for you, are not going well,

'Twill likely make you mad as hell.

Just keep in mind that 'twon't take long,

For you to RIGHT this pesky wrong.

Temptation is to moan and groan,

In this you will not be alone.

But keep in mind if you get mad,

You just may lose the chance you had

To fix the problem right away,

But miss it and you'll rue the day.

The best way to your foes beguile,

Just take your lumps and smile, smile, smile.

Some clever bright song-writing fella

Said, "let a smile be your umbrella."

Though it may take a little while,

Things WILL go better with a smile.

It takes fewer muscles to smile than to scowl. There's a message here.

SOMEDAY

These poems may some day be unfurled,

In many places `round the world.

And people will most likely ask,

Why did you undertake this task?

These poems touch on such varied themes,

Depicting many different scenes.

They touch on people, places, things,

Ideas fly on verbal wings.

There's good advice for girl and boy,

Which even parents will enjoy.

I hope you like the thoughts and style,

And trust you find them worth your while.

Illustration of an old steam engine on wooden skids.

By Heather Brown

STARTING OUT

Footloose and carefree right here in B.C.,
Seeking adventure, the right place to be.
Meeting new people from so many lands,
No shortage of work for strong willing hands.
My buddy and I, we just could not fail,
Luck of the Irish, the world by the tail.
We heard about jobs, in Coast logging camps,
A good place to be, for travelling tramps,
Where loggers worked hard, far out in the bush,
Being run by a boss, best known as the "Push".
Chokermen, chasers and head-loaders too
And other strange titles, made up the crew.
Fallers and buckers were all on the list,
Mechanics and welders cannot be missed.
Drillers and blasters were men among men,
Blew many a bear, right out of its den.
There were cat skinners and drivers of trucks,
All with ambition to make the big bucks.
There was no problem to line up a job,
Sign on the line, you are one of the mob.
Get on the ship to our Camp up the Coast,
Pioneer Timber, your welcoming host.
Nose to the grindstone, just give it your best,
Show up for work, we'll take care of the rest.
There was a constant turnover of crew,
Lots of good chances to learn something new.
We joined the ranks of experienced men
And never signed out as two greenhorns again.

STAY OUTTA THE BIGHT

The chalkboard in the window said it all,
Come in, this is the Logger's hiring hall.
We're hiring for our camps along the Coast,
Alaska Pine would like to be your host.
The Union steamship sails tomorrow night,
We need some husky loggers sharp and bright.
So if you'll sign along this dotted line
You'll be among the finest of the fine.
We only log in daylight not in dark
And where we log is much like Stanley Park,
So if it's fame and fortune that you seek
We hope you'll stay for more than just a week.
We're sending you to work in Port McNeill,
It's just the kind of place that makes you feel
That if you really want to learn to log
And you are not inclined to duck the fog,
You might stay 'round and get to know the ropes
And see how loggers log those forest slopes.
You'll need a hardhat, Stanfields and caulk boots,
In case it rains, one of them slicker suits.
This prepaid ticket lets you board the ship
You'll embark at the Union Steamship slip.
You've got yourself a one-way ticket cruise
And a special way of life, you cannot lose.
Now as you leave this useless city strife
And take your first steps to a logger's life
There's a fifty-fifty chance you'll stay the course
And if you do you'll surely be a force,
So work hard and get used to doings things right,
And heed old Moore's advice, stay outta the bight.

My good friend Bill Moore ran his own logging camp in Downtown Winter Harbour on the North West tip of Vancouver Island. He liked to write poetry and always finished letters, articles and meetings with the admonishment, "stay outta the bight".

STEPPING CAREFULLY

How you step, where you step, when you step,

Choosing the right step, can save your life.

Tying up an oil tanker to a narrow slippery dock

After nightfall, requires very careful steps.

Climbing up and down ladders on thirty foot high tanks

Being pumped full, requires more careful steps

And is almost as dangerous as jumping

From one tank top to another in driving rain.

Doing the work myself because I could not sleep

If I knew that one of my crew

Was out there risking his life, alone.

When all the right steps have been taken,

The tanks are full, I cast off the tanker.

I take the last few precarious steps

To shut off the pipeline valves,

Where the dock meets the steep shoreline.

An eerie silence, as the first light of day

Peers dimly through the early morning mist

Rolling up the beach.

Watching my step as I stand on the pipelines.

Continued………

Continued.........

I turn the wheel valves to close them.

I hear the clip, clop, clip, clop of cloven feet

As a mother deer and her fawn

Come trotting towards me,

About ten feet from the water's edge,

Running in water and leaving no scent

For some prowling early-morn cougar

Looking for his breakfast........

Now that's stepping carefully.

I take the last few tired steps

To my pickup and clip my seat-belt

Before I start my engine,

Thinking of cougars

And breakfast.

The idea for this poem came as I stood precariously on the fuel pipelines, about ten feet above the beach at the end of our wharf. I had been working all night, unloading an oil barge, and was conscious of the care needed to step carefully on the pipelines as I shut and locked the valves. Then a deer and fawn came clip-clopping along the beach, running in the water to avoid leaving a scent and becoming a cougar's breakfast. Ah yes, time for breakfast.

SUCCESS STORY

By

John Allemang

The bottom line? Betrayal works.
Ex-CEOs must have their perks,
And if you're David Emerson,
There's no way that you ever run
For Parliament, unless you know
You'll net a decent quid pro quo.

It's fine to talk of loyalty,
But when you're business royalty,
High office has to be your due,
So changing into Tory blue,
And turning enemies to friends,
Is simply how a man ascends.

They jeered him when he crossed the floor?
That's just the Commons phony war,
Which needn't occupy the mind
Once Ottawa is left behind,
And Stephen Harper's superstar
Can lord it over Kandahar.

Good thing he's not still with the Grits-
Yes, Opposition is the pits,
But truthfully, he's no Bob Rae,
While set beside Maxime Bernier,
That Judas, David Emerson,
Becomes, somehow, the Chosen One.

(Reprinted with the kind permission of the Globe & Mail with thanks to John Allemang and Celia Donnelly.) See next page.

SUCCESS STORY...A RIPOSTE

"NEVER SEND A BOY TO DO A MAN'S JOB"

John Allemang decries success,
In true tradition of the press.
He wrote a poem as a joke,
At David Emerson, a poke.
Prime Minister is also named,
Just doing his job, why's he defamed?

He's given Emerson the task,
Foreign Affairs, a lot to ask.
With challenges on every side
And Dave accepted it with pride.
His duties will be carried out.
No secret papers lying about.

His style is noted for aplomb,
A star in Stephen's Cabinet Room.
So Editor, my plea to you,
Is to give credit where it's due.
Ignore your poet's crass assault,
Prime Minister is not at fault.

Confronted by the Afghan strife,
Our troops are there, each risks his life.
Aware of all those lives to save,
Our Leader sends his best man Dave.
The honest truth, let's not be coy,
When it's men's work, don't send a boy.

*When Prime Minister Stephen Harper appointed former Liberal David Emerson to serve
as Canada's Foreign Affairs Minister, John Allemang of the Globe & Mail wrote a tongue-in-
cheek poem. I wrote a riposte which John humorously acknowledged.*

Two loggers taking a prisoner

See next page

TAKE LOTS MORE PRISONERS

The life was tough in every logging camp,

In winter we complained about the damp.

In summer our big challenge was to beat,

No-see-ums, big mosquitoes and the heat.

Each morning we would don our bone-dry suits,

Put on the regulation spiked caulk boots.

Climbed aboard a crew-bus just like cattle,

Feeling much like soldiers off to battle.

To make each log a prisoner of our crew,

It was the job that we were paid to do.

Each prisoner was choked and hauled away,

With luck, at least a hundred every day.

That was the daily routine of our lives,

The work on which our Forest business thrives.

The business pays a gross amount of tax,

A lot of heavy pressure on our backs.

And so, our Province really has it good,

Our most important export is that wood.

Without it our economy would fail,

And that's the reason for this little tale.

TAKING CARE

Unseemly as it is to boast,

For certain if you are the host.

There are some things we should not do,

So here's a poem to remind you

That it's not cool to show your wealth

Or claim that you're in perfect health.

You may indeed be very rich

And have all kinds of money which

Puts you among the wealthy few,

Time on your hands, naught else to do.

This is the time to be aware

How urgent 'tis to take good care

Of mind and body's basic health,

Without it, what's the good of wealth?

Beach Camp

This camp was built to house the drivers and mechanics who hauled iron ore from the Merry Widow Mountain iron mine and for the crew that maintained the feeders, stackers and conveyor systems that stored the ore and loaded the ships. The Norwegian manager of the Mine was Alf Ostergaard who was concerned at the lack of a good maintenance program at Beach Camp and hired an old pal of his to be the Foreman. His name was Danny Sedor. I worked for the trucking company, Reynolds Transportation Ltd., that hauled the ore as well as mooring, loading and casting off the deep-sea cargo ships. Danny had some run-ins with the American who ran that Company. I was sometimes the meat in the sandwich when they disagreed, which was often.

I wrote a poem for Danny and gave it to his wife. It made her laugh. They moved away the following year and I never saw them again. I had not kept a copy of the poem and forgot all about it, until one day many years later; two ladies came to the Port McNeill Town Office. They were daughters of the Sedors and had found the poem in Mrs. Sedor's souvenirs after she and Danny had passed away. They had typed up the poem from my hand-written version and wanted to deliver it personally to me. Unfortunately, I was in Victoria and did not meet them.

It was very gracious of them to bring me the copy and I am delighted to include it in this book in memory of their father and mother.

Continued………

THE BEACH CAMP

You might think that we never have problems 'round here,

But spare me a minute, just lend me your ear.

Our job as you know is to load up the ships,

Exporting ore to the land of the Nips.

Well, throughout the first three years on the job,

We had Supers galore as part of the mob,

Haywire mechanics and men who could log,

One thing about them, they could all duck the fog.

The big brain came down from the camp at the Mine,

And said, "Vy the hell do tings not go so fine?

The party must finish, I'm ending the fun,

I'm sending to town for a son-of-a-gun.

Whenever my troubles and woes are too many,

I phone up Vancouver and get my friend Danny.

He'll be here in a week to clean up the mess,

But how he will do it is anyone's guess."

When Danny arrived, he said to his Mrs.,

"I've never seen any place quite like this is."

His Mrs. Replied with a frown on her face,

"It won't be too long, I'll be leaving this place."

Well Danny went out and began like a tank,

But found his way blocked by a tough looking Yank,

Who said, "while you're here, regard me as the boss.

As Canada's gain is America's loss."

Continued........

Continued.........

But Danny tried hard and to work was his aim,

If nothing got done then the Yank was to blame.

There were no spare parts and no welding rod,

"Get them" said Danny, "or I'm quitting by God!"

So the Yank saw the light and got Danny a raise,

The first time they'd spoken for quite a few days.

He ordered the parts that were needed from town,

And since then, there never has been a breakdown.

We load many ships now, they oft stand in line,

But the loading is done in the quickest of time.

No sooner they tie up beneath our big spout,

There's a whir and a bang and the ore's falling out.

Yes, we're loading them fast now, the big and the small,

And soon we'll be loading the biggest of all.

Twenty-four thousand tons they want in one load,

Five hundred trips for the trucks on the road.

And when she is loaded, you'll hear the men boast,

Of the greatest ship-loading along the West Coast.

In the thick of it all is the man with the tools,

Pushing his crew to work like damn fools.

Scowling and growling and wearing a frown,

Making his name as a man of renown.

Our Danny will be there earning his gravy,

Sinking more tonnage than anyone's navy.

For the daughters of Mr. & Mrs. Dan Sedor

THE DIVINER

There is a talent that's divine,

A talent that's hard to define.

There are not many with that gift,

Whose reputation gets a lift

By finding water with a stick.

I do not jest, this is no trick.

One cuts a forked branch off a tree

Then snips the leaves `til it's leaf free.

It's firmly held, a fork each hand,

Walked back and forth across the land.

The stick's pulled down with all its might,

The witcher's got to hold on tight.

He marks a spot, the pull is strong.

It's rare to find a witcher wrong.

The question then, how much, how deep.

To drill a well does not come cheap.

Some use a pendulum to tell,

How deep, productive, is each well.

And for this magic occupation,

There's no simple explanation.

I use a forked branch of an Alder tree and it is almost pulled out of my hands by the "magical" pull that is created when over a potential source of well water.

136

THE EMPEROR'S CLOTHES

An Emperor in days gone by,
Was well-known for his need to try
On different kinds of fancy clothes.
What was the reason, no-one knows.
His courtiers all expressed their awe
At every new outfit they saw,
In velvet, wool and even silk,
All pleased the sycophantic ilk.

Then one day, appeared a vision,
The Emperor, was it derision?
Attended at a big State Ball,
With not a stitch of clothes at all.
The sycophants showed no surprise
On seeing their leader in this guise.
They shouted out, "Olay! Olay!
Just see how well he's dressed today."

Until a boy in innocence,
To whom these actions made no sense,
Shouted in a voice so loud,
The bravest one in all the crowd.
"Our leader is plain naked, stark,"
Then all the dogs began to bark
And with no further ifs or buts,
The crowd began to shout, "he's nuts."

Continued………

Continued.........

"Oh look, oh look, how sad, how sad,

It seems our leader has gone mad."

'Tis sad, none of his faithful minions,

Could express their true opinions.

They took the Emperor away,

And placed him in the Royal sick-bay,

Where he was locked up safe and sound,

With only padded walls around.

It is a fact, still true today,

Most people are afraid to say,

What's really on their thoughtful minds?

Instead they sit on their behinds.

So we should not be scared to shout,

If in our hearts we have some doubt,

About the things our leaders say,

In trying to lead us day by day.

Inspired by a story by Hans Christian Andersen, famous Danish writer (1805-1875)

THE EYES HAVE IT

For fashion's sake, some people take

A certain type of clothes,

And don't realize, that in this guise,

They should not choose to pose.

If they have cash, they'll make a dash

And spend it if they can,

New suit and hat, not knowing that,

Clothes do not make the man.

But should such rake, a moment take,

To think about this fact.

To me and you, it's what we do,

When friends see how we act.

We can beguile with just a smile,

No matter what we wear.

'Tis in our eyes our kindness lies,

Where we show how we care.

So if we should, try to look good,

Our eyes complete the role.

We should realize, that our two eyes

Are windows of our soul.

THE FIRST

Think of the adventures you've had,

The pleasant, the good and the bad.

There's one that should clearly stand out,

About which you do not have doubt.

And if you can handle the truth,

It ended the days of your youth.

Your innocence vanished that night,

A moment of fleeting delight.

That first time you'll never forget

The person who lovingly let

You have that sweet moment of bliss

Which started with one little kiss.

There may have been others since then,

But none like the first time again.

And whether you're pauper or prince,

You've dwelt on that memory since.

It matters not how you may thirst,

There'll never again be a first.

THE GARAGE SALE

A sign with little arrows showed the way

It simply said "Garage Sale here today".

We wondered at the kind of person who

Would sell the garage and not the house too.

The arrows led us to a milling crowd,

With lively music played through speakers loud.

We drove a block to find a place to park

Where someone owned a dog that liked to bark

At all the strangers who were walking 'round

His sidewalk and his private piece of ground.

We walked back down the narrow crowded street

And saw the owner standing there discreet.

Beside him stood a harried looking wife

Amidst the private details of their life.

On tables, shelves and boxes neatly laid

All kinds of household items were displayed.

With pictures, books and records all for sale,

Some clubs and racquets, golf balls by the pail.

The crowd were buying, loading up their cars.

One lady bought a crate of pickling jars.

Most of them packed so many things away

They'll have enough for their own sale some day.

THE GREAT MUSHROOM HUNT

The thought was great, we won't sleep late.
We'll rise at crack of dawn
And leave the house, quiet as a mouse,
By sun-up we'll be gone.
We had a plan, sure that we can
Bring home some mushrooms wild.
So off we biked, the way we liked,
The morning clear and mild.
There was no doubt, we'd heard about
A well-known mushroom field.
We could not rest, we had to test
To see what it would yield.
So, not too late, we reached the gate
No mushrooms could be seen.
There was no white, anywhere in sight,
The field was a sea of green.
Tom gave a smile, said "wait a while,
The sun is warming up.
And when it's high, up in the sky.
Of 'shrooms there'll be enough."
So we sat there, in silent prayer,
Doubts building in our minds,
Upon that fence, our feelings tense,
A pain in our behinds.
It took an hour, our minds now dour,
For us to realise,
There was no way, we'd 'shroom that day,
We were two stupid guys.
So off we go our spirits low
And bike the ten miles home.
No 'shrooms in hand, sad memories and
An interesting poem!

Within a few miles of where we lived in Cork, we heard there was a field which produced large amounts of mushrooms. It was a few miles beyond White's Cross and would take us an hour to get there on our bikes. We wanted to be sure that we got there early, which meant leaving home at daybreak. We didn't bother with breakfast because we thought that we'd be home quickly with the mushrooms. The poem tells the rest of the story.

THE HEIRLOOM?

There was a logger whom we knew as Max

Who always packed a very special axe.

It had been in his family many years

And losing it, one of his greatest fears.

He worked so hard the handles did not last

It's had a dozen handles in the past.

The axe-head always sharp and working well,

Was changed more oft' than anyone can tell.

It's nice this little story to recall,

But was it such an heirloom after all?

THE LADY OF THE RED ROOM, BELFAST.

A wild overgrown garden, a house that has seen better days,
On a once quiet residential street near the University,
Being slowly overtaken by progress and commerce.
She sits in stately grandeur
With the perfect poise
Of the ballet-dancer she always was,
In a jumble of relics and mementoes
In a sea of red.
Red cushions, red chairs, red toys, and even red walls.
The phrase, "I love you,"
Is on many of the heart-shaped cushions,
In memory, perhaps, of the death of a young son,
One of the three apples of her eye.
All of whom she loved so dearly,
And the earlier death of a young husband,
Both long before their time.
Remembering another son and a daughter,
Who seem to have forgotten the lady of the red room.
Memories flood back of happier and better times
And violent ones too when the Troubles were at their peak.
Only the Irish could come up with a word,
Such an innocuous word as, "Troubles,"
To describe a nation struggling for freedom and independence.
Memories of a sound like a backfire,
Which was a bomb exploding second next door,
And covering the dismembered body of her neighbour
With a white sheet, which turned quickly to red.
The poise and grace and beauty of the ballet-dancer,
Is still evident in the frail body
With a backbone of steel,
And an indomitable spirit and strength within,
Red is such a strong colour.
It suits the Lady of the Red Room.

Dedicated to a life-long friend of mine from Cork who settled in Belfast and maintained a calm attitude during the years of the "troubles".

THE LAND OF A TRILLION TREES

The folks who live here will be heard to boast,

Of the life they lead on B.C.'s Wild West coast.

With the ocean out in front and woods behind,

With Mother Nature often harsh, yet kind.

Where mountains penetrate the passing clouds

And islands hide where rolling fog enshrouds,

Where deer and bear and cougars freely roam

And Orca "whales" and dolphins make their home.

Where folks from all of nature's human clan,

Live lives of peace beside their fellow man,

Where sun and rain and healthy ocean breeze,

Bless all who live in this land of a trillion trees.

Starting in the nineteen eighties, an anti-logging campaign crept into British Columbia from the U.S.A. It was funded by wealthy foundations and seriously affected our forestry-dependent communities. It was a sad time to be the Mayor of a logging town like ours. We knew how valuable our contributions were to the provincial and national economy, but even our own governments seemed by their inaction, to be against us. A twisted anti-logging campaign was claiming that within ten or twelve years there would be no forests left in British Columbia. On the drive back up Island from a pro-logging rally, I tried to calculate how many trees there were growing here by extrapolating acres of land under forestry and the numbers of trees that grow on each acre. Even the ditches on the highway were clogged with trees. This poem was written on that journey home.

"THE LEGAL GAME"

There is a group of legalistic folk

About whom all the rest of us will joke.

They're educated in the country's laws,

They'll analyze them for you clause by clause.

They speak a legal language to confuse

The rest of us when we don't share their views.

They've built the justice system to control

Each one of us, regardless of our role.

Consultations charged out by the minute,

Costs build up real fast, there is no limit.

And if you ever have to go to Court,

You'll see that this law game is just a sport.

There's lawyers on each side, sometimes a team,

Their arguments at times are quite extreme.

Their game is played to entertain the judge

Who sits their looking serious, nudge nudge.

They call each other names like "learned friend"

And plead their case with fervour to the end.

The judge pays some attention to each side

So they can look professional with pride.

Some times he'll ask them to approach the bench

Where they will talk in whispers and entrench.

I've looked at these short sessions with a hunch

And figured that they were just planning lunch.

THE LESSON

He landed in camp, was willing to work,
Well-educated, a bit of a jerk.
Passed his exams with a ninety percent,
Sharp as a tack, quite the young gent.
Ready for work and to do what 'twould take,
Work through the summer to save him a stake.
Born with a big silver spoon in his mouth,
This was no average logging camp lout.
Hungry for money he put in the time
And worked like a slave to make every dime.
When payday arrived he had lots of cash
And wanted to find ways to add to his stash.
He heard that the cook was needing a loan,
Wife and her boyfriend were losing their home.

So, down the boardwalk to talk to the cook,
Offered a loan which he wrote in his book.
He said he would charge a mere ten percent,
Covering the cost of the money he lent.
Four weeks to the day, the cook paid him back,
Over a drink in the warmth of his shack.
Throughout the summer he loaned him again,
Always while charging his percentage ten.
The total increased to meet the cook's need,
While caution and care were savaged by greed.
As winter winds were beginning to blow,
The cook needed more, he could not say no.
He lent him the works down to his last cent
And never again saw that food-swilling gent.

One summer, a recently graduated university student arrived in camp to work. He was a bit of a know-it-all who thought that he could make some extra money by loaning cash to any would-be borrowers. This poem describes his experience as a one-man bank and the problems that can affect any banker.

THE MEETING PLACE

I wake up each morning with sharp hunger pangs

And that's where the gist of this little rhyme hangs.

It's normal to feel like some bacon and eggs

With mugs of strong coffee right down to the dregs.

For loggers and miners who work in the bush

'Tis common to start off the day with some mush,

And crews of the fish boats and hard working tugs

Are never too far from their hot coffee mugs,

But there is a breakfast which I prefer most,

A stop at BoBanee's for great raisin toast.

Washed down with hot coffee and endless refills,

That heart warming nectar fills me to the gills.

There's other great choices that make up their list.

Their Mexican dishes just should not be missed.

And if you should feel like a really good lunch,

There's all sorts of choices on which you can munch.

At dinnertime they serve a really good meal,

The prices are right, as there's no better deal.

The staff are a great bunch and have lots of style

And they will greet you with a welcoming smile.

So if you are hungry and feel, like a feed,

A meal at Bo-Banee's will please every need.

Written for a well-known restaurant in Port McNeill and its cheerful staff.

THE MENTOR

It's time to consider, size up and address
The reason that some folks are such a success.
So many work hard and yet never make it,
Others are lucky they reach out and take it.
It's hard to define and pin down how it works,
As failure so often 'round each corner lurks.
We tend to attribute a lot to plain luck
But that's not how Gretsky ends up with the puck.
With practice and skill he was able to see
Not where the puck was, but more likely to be.
There's one other factor we tend to ignore
And that is the mentor who helps us to score.
The help of such mentor outweighs all the rest,
His guidance provides us the spur to be best.
A mentor is there throughout every season,
It's hard to explain or think of a reason
But if you're lucky and meet such a mentor
Just open your mind and bid him to enter.
Now during my life I have sometimes been blessed
With leaders who led far ahead of the rest.
In Ireland 'twas Jack O', in London J. Keane,
In B.C. 'twas Horace, shop foreman supreme.
Then came a junction that led to success.
My bid for Shell Agent, Art Sanford said "yes",
His simple decision, thus opened the way
That started the business we run to this day.

Success is often dependent on luck, or just being in the right place at the right time. It also helps if you meet and recognize the value of a mentor. My first boss in Cork when I left school was a very successful Chartered Accountant called Jack O'Connor for whom I worked for three years. My next mentor was a department Manager in Fords in Dagenham near London, England. He ran the tractor and truck manufacturing division in a huge factory that was a square mile in area. His name was Gerry Keane, OBE. (That's Order of the British Empire, awarded for running a factory that was attacked regularly by German bombers during the War). My first Canadian mentor was Horace Arthurs, the Master Mechanic at Pioneer Timber, Port McNeill. He is the main reason I stayed in Port McNeill. He wrote a great book on logging called "The Last Wooden Spar". An Old-Country gentleman called Art Sanford selected me from a bunch of applicants, to represent Shell Canada in the North Island, in June 1961. There have been many others, but these four were pivotal.

THE MIDNIGHT SWIM

This is the story of a man called Ted,

A hard-working miner, very well fed.

Never missed a meal, never showed up late

Packed a double lunch, very over-weight.

Worked on the grizzly, dumping loads of ore,

Eighteen loads a shift, sometimes even more

Lived in the bunkhouse, with the ore-haul crew.

One winter evening, not too much to do,

A bunch of the guys, were sitting around.

"Let's take Deanie's boat, get beer parlour bound,

A half an hour will get us to the Bay,

A perfect way to end the working day."

They made it to the Bay in half an hour,

The diesel engine working at full power.

By midnight they had had enough to drink,

Climbed back on board just loaded to the brink.

Old Teddy was the last to climb aboard.

As soon as he was on, the engine roared.

They huddled in the galley, sipping beer,

The ocean fairly calm and weather clear.

Got back to Camp, all keen to get to bed,

But soon realized that they had lost old Ted.

One of the lads had seen him going aft,

To pee away the beer that he had quaffed.

They headed back, switched on the big spot-light,

Ten minutes sailing, Ted hove into sight.

Continued........

Continued………

They could not lift him up and o'er the side,

Too water-logged, had too much to imbibe.

The best that they could do, was tie a rope,

Around his torso, 'twas the only hope,

They towed him back to Camp along the shore,

At least a two mile tow and maybe more.

They beached him on the barge-ramp, like a whale,

Six pairs of muscled arms just could not fail.

They loaded him back on to Deanie's boat,

Wrapped up in blankets and a heavy coat.

Sailed to the Hospital, back at the Bay,

Met doctor and the nurse, at break of day.

The hypothermia took some time to cure,

Hot baths aplenty had Ted clean and pure.

Ted got back to Camp, the following morn,

Feeling much better, a miner reborn.

Such an adventure was nothing to him,

He claimed he enjoyed his first midnight swim.

The ore haul truckers lived in a small bunkhouse and cookhouse complex at Beach Camp, Port McNeill. The ore was hauled in belly-dump trailers from the Merry Widow Mine over a rough and hazardous gravel haul road. These were dumped into a grizzly at Beach Camp and the ore was stacked by a system of conveyor belts. One night, on my second load, I arrived at the grizzly and Helmut the night dump-man was nowhere to be seen. I looked around for him and he finally came panting up the hill from the beach where I could see the lights of a Gillnetter and people running around with flashlights. He told me that Teddy, the daytime dump-man had fallen off the stern of the Gillnetter on the trip back from Alert Bay, where some of the day-shift crew had gone for a beer. Teddy would never again try to relieve himself from such a precarious urinal as the stern of a Gillnetter in rough weather.

THE ONE, THE ONLY

The menu says "Since 1912"

This makes me curious to delve,

Why in this sleazy part of town

This famous caf' has not shut down.

The puzzle is how it's held out

Where people live from hand to mouth.

The nearby streets saw better days

Where now the drunk and druggy sways.

On every side, such awful waste,

Where once life used to be fast paced.

Next door was once the Hiring Hall

Where companies both large and small

Hired crews for coastal logging shows

When e'er the price of lumber rose.

Today it's really sad to see

These streets the scene of misery.

The people in some drug-caused rut,

The buildings mostly boarded shut.

In the midst of all this squalor

Just one place that makes a dollar.

The café best known as just "The Only",

Looks run down and very lonely.

Two well-worn counters, metal stools,

Two simple booths, one waitress rules.

Continued........

Continued........

A place where once big deals were made,

Saw politicians every shade,

M.P.'s and M.L.A.'s and lo,

Its best-known patron Pierre Trudeau.

They came for special meals of fish,

A magic touch to every dish.

It may be poached, range-grilled or fried,

In golden batter, fish inside.

Amazing chowder by the bowl,

With crackers, toast or crusty roll.

If you want another reason,

Try their fish-cheeks when in season.

We ate there first in '56,

The day we signed out for the sticks,

And every time we came to Town,

We hit this place of great renown.

It's still a cookin' every day,

Well worth a visit, need I say,

Do not dress up, you should dress down

Should you visit this part of Town.

Since 1912 a Café called "The Only" has consistently served the best fish dishes in Vancouver at West Hastings Street, near Carrall Street. I have been going there since my first meal there in June 1956. The quality is still there though the premises and surrounding streets are a bit rundown. I had lunch there recently. The place was busy with a motley clientele; a couple of businessmen in suits, a guy with a wheeled suitcase who looked as if he had just got in from Ottawa, a disheveled street person and two guys in a booth doing a drug deal. There is no public toilet as they were not required to provide one in 1912. It's a very small place. So "go" before you go. It is well worth the visit.

THE SAGA OF TELEGRAPH COVE

I have a real strong urge to tell,
The story of old Fred Wastell,
A man who stood above the crowd,
A man who made his family proud.
Soon after Fred saw light of day,
The family moved to Alert Bay,
Up near the top of Johnstone Straits,
Where he developed business traits.
The major industry was fish,
In cans, or salted, as you wish,
Shipped out in boxes made of wood.
To own a sawmill would be good.
So Fred set up a mill and staff,
Tucked in the Cove of Telegraph.
Deliveries all were made by sea,
Upon his boat, the Gikumi.
It towed the logs in to the mill,
Then moving lumber was the drill.
The costs were low, the business straight,
His name and reputation great.
It kept Fred and the sawmill crew,
With almost too much work to do.
That wood built mines and logging camps,
Workshops, wharves and access ramps.
Alex McDonald was his pard,
Who kept the mill crew working hard,
As Fred around the district rove,
Selling that lumber from the Cove.
The local mines produced much ore,
Twelve ships a year and sometimes more.
In stormy weather they would need
A line boat and a tug to lead
Them safely to the loading dock,
Where Fred would stand by 'round the clock,
While handling all the work on deck,
Was Jimmy Burton at his beck.

Continued.........

154

Continued........

Now sometimes on a sunny day,
They'd sail across to Alert Bay,
To pick up fuel and food and worse,
They'd invite each off-duty nurse,
To join them for a day at sea
As long as they would make the tea,
The sandwiches and things for lunch,
So Fred and Jim had things to munch.
The girls enjoyed the fine cuisine
And always left the galley clean.
Those happy times are now long gone,
Since Fred, some years ago passed on.
The mill has closed, the workers left,
But yet the place is not bereft.
The Cove has now become the place,
To live life at a slower pace.
A place you will not soon forget,
With restaurant and rooms to let.
Whale watching, fishing, kayaks too,
Give visitors so much to do.
So take a moment, stop and greet,
Gord Graham is the man to meet.
He's always pleased to stop and talk,
Striding along the Cove's boardwalk.
A chat with him will let you see
Why the Cove is the place to be.
And it is likely Gord will tell,
It's all because of Fred Wastell.

For many years there was no road to Telegraph Cove, even though it was potentially within minutes of Beaver Cove and Kokish. Eventually the logging camp managers who formed the majority on the local School Board decided "logger fashion" to "slap in a road" so they could bus the Telegraph Cove kids to the school at Kokish and shut down the little school at Telegraph Cove. The mill produced lumber for all the local communities which was delivered by Fred Wastell on his seine-boat-sized tug-come lumber carrier, the M/V Gikumi. My wife and I made many trips with him around the Broughton Archipelago delivering lumber, and got to know him really well when he acted as pilot boat and tug-boat when he serviced the iron-ore and copper ships that came to Port McNeill to load for foreign ports.

A view of Telegraph Cove with a boom of logs waiting for the sawmill.

The M/V Gikumi is moored at the dock below Fred Wastell's house.

THE TRIALS AND TRIBULATIONS OF A LOGGING CAMP COOK

Author unknown

A hustling man will rise at morn,
Before the rooster blows his horn,
But I am here to tell about,
The guy who calls the rooster out,
THE COOK, the foolish hard-worked slave,
Whose duty is to drudge and save,
Who seeks his weary bed with sighs,
And meets himself about to rise.
A Cook who is a real live-wire,
Will rise at four to light the fire,
So that the coffee and the mush,
Will boil up fine without a rush,
And that each hungry lumberjack,
Will get his bacon and his stack
Of hotcakes served so steaming hot,
They'd scorch the gullet of a sot.
Now when this morning meal is o'er,
And he has laboured on since four,
You'd think perhaps the fool just might,
Take time to grab himself a bite,
But if he does 'tis on the jump,
For he must stir himself and hump,
And do a thousand irksome things,
Before he hears the bell that rings
To call the loggers in at noon,
Alas the time comes all too soon.
And now I'll make a little sketch,
Of how he does that forenoon stretch
In every week of labour hard,
So that each logger and his pard
May stuff himself at that noon meal,
And ne'r a bad effect may feel.

Continued........

Continued………

First thing he does is set the punk,
And that itself is quite a chunk.
Mixing it is sure a chore,
A washtub full and flowing o'er.
To keep the dough from getting cold
He kneads it well and puts in mould
A half a hundred loaves or so,
And all the rolls that with it go.
Then he must rush and cut the meat
And fix it up so nice and neat.
He puts it on to fry or roast
While hands and feet are hot as toast,
With all the heat that radiates
From ovens and from frying plates.
He turns from this with sigh on sigh
And hustles 'round to make the pie.
Thirty pies he makes galore,
A pie a minute is his score.
The logger will not use his hand,
To eat it like the ill-bred band.
He would not for his very life
He knows enough to use his knife.
And then perhaps he has a whim,
That pie is not enough for him,
So puddings rich with sauce or fruit,
The cook must make for him to boot.
Every time he turns about,
He finds that he has just run out
Of cookies, cakes and jellyroll,
And other things that loggers bold,
Demand with curse and hungry look,
We'll have them - Sir - or can the cook.

Continued………

Continued.........

Cook keeps on from morn 'til night,

Next day is in the same old plight.

The flunkies stand around and shirk,

And leave the cook to do the work.

The second gets his little pay

On false pretenses day to day.

The bullcook thinks the joke is good,

If he can cheat him on the wood.

And if the logger gets his fill

The boss will say there's too much swill.

But if by chance he makes her pay,

The logger like an ass will bray.

So now - my friends - just let me tell,

Take a sporting chance on hell.

Be a knave or be a crook,

But NEVER, NEVER be a COOK.

I originally heard this poem recited by a gentlemanly logger named Dick Rydeen who did not know who wrote it and who did not have a written version of the poem. I made notes as he recited it and I have rounded out the bits I was not too sure about. Whoever wrote the original version had to have been a logging-camp cook. The word "punk" seems to describe the first step in bread making, and "mould" probably refers to "yeast". I would appreciate any information that a reader may have on this poem. The first eight lines are classic.

THE WINE MENU

Superlatives describing wine

Use words like, tasty, rich, sublime.

The writers do not hesitate

To boast and yes, exaggerate.

Their adjectives to palates please,

Are tossed around with clever ease.

Words like awesome, rich and stunning,

Indicate a certain cunning.

To sell the sizzle, not the steak,

Which means we should a moment take,

To analyse the words they use,

As they promote their vinous booze.

Like toasty, rich, mouth-filling, clean,

Superb, fantastic, and supreme,

Deluxe, demanding and first rate,

You'll love this wine, as will your mate.

Accept our words, keen to a fault,

Best taken with a grain of salt.

Reading a wine menu on a British Airways flight to London inspired me to write this poem.
Wine menus are written by people who have the greatest collection of adjectives and are
not slow or shy to use them. As they say, "enjoy!"

THERE'S NO SUCH WORD AS "CAN'T"

I once worked in a coastal logging camp,

In circumstances that were cold and damp,

The challenges we faced were so diverse,

They ranged across the board from bad to worse.

With tangled rigging, hang-ups and breakdowns,

We soon became accustomed to the sounds

Of screaming foremen out to make 'er pay,

Just trying to get the most from every day.

And there were times when problems loomed so large,

The God of Hopeless Cases was in charge.

Temptation was, to say "it can't be done",

So clearly, in the minds of everyone.

But that's when you would hear the loggers rant,

We just do not accept a word like "can't".

To fix this problem may not be much fun,

But just like all the others, "twill be done"!

THESE FOLKS WHO MAKE OUR COUNTRY STRONG

In conversation with a friend of mine,

He said he'd love to see a simple rhyme.

He touched upon a fact that made me think,

It's time to take some paper, pen & ink

And recognise the heroes in our midst.

The more I thought, the longer went the list.

The concept was to skip the Hall of Fame

And list the unsung heroes in life's game.

We tend to take for granted all they do,

Without them, it would just be me and you.

They tend to work away behind the scenes,

Adapting to the seasons and the themes.

You'll see them in the bleachers, every game,

The sport may change, the faces are the same.

Coaching soccer games, helping at the pool,

For special projects, they'll be at the school.

They work, they pay their taxes and they vote.

They read their local paper and take note

On how their town or province is being run.

If they're not satisfied they'll be the one

To let the politicians know they care,

In voicing their opinions they've no fear.

They quietly go about their daily lives,

Because of them our country really thrives.

So if you have the time to go along,

Join with these folks who make our country strong.

Written for, and dedicated to, our volunteers. Suggested by my good friends, Eric and Jeannie Tegelberg.

"THEY" IS "YOU"

I never cease to be amazed
At issues that are often raised
By people who prefer to vent
Against the folks in government.
One wonders where they get the gall,
As they do not take part at all
In politics of any kind
And do not ever get behind
The people who each day must make
The tough decisions it will take
To govern for the common good.
These critics, if they wanted could,
Run for election, take a stand
Help to govern this great land.
If they think what this about is
Put their money where their mouth is.
They'll soon realize it's very hard
To please each person and his pard.
Though you may do your very best
You'll please just some, offend the rest.
Though you may wish, as so do I,
You can't please all, though you may try.
Complaints will be heard every day
And start out with some unknown "they"
"They" should do this, "they" should do that,
That unknown "they", is where it's at.
The basic fact, of course is true
'Cause you is "they" and "they" is you.
Next time you hear some critic wail
Read out to him this simple tale.

THOSE WHO CAN, DO. THOSE WHO CAN'T, CRITICIZE.

I tend to take a lot of joy

From efforts of a girl or boy,

Whose talents show in works of art,

In music when they play a part.

It may be in the written word,

Or in a song their voice is heard,

Their talent may be in a sport,

A champion on the tennis court.

They may be actors on a stage,

Pretending joy or even rage.

There is a fact that they should know,

That there are critics at each show.

And though they may have won a prize,

It's sad, but they must realize

That there are those who could, but don't,

As criticizing is their wont.

So those with egos large in size,

Inept themselves, will critize.

THUNDER AND LIGHTNING.

Last night I lay me down to sleep in bed,

The night-light in the corner glowing red.

My brother in his bed across the room,

Lay snoring quietly in the midnight gloom.

When suddenly the room was bright as day

A lightning flash from not too far away.

Followed by the noise of crashing thunder.

Lying there quite scared, it made me wonder.

Another lightning flash and thunder clap,

`Twas loud but did not spoil my brother's nap.

And as I lay there wide, so wide awake,

I realized this was too much to take.

I left the safety of my cozy room

As lightning flashed, another thunder boom.

I gently tapped upon my parent's door

And told them I was scared, could take no more.

I climbed into their bed so safe and warm

With Mom and Dad my life was back to norm.

Dedicated to my brother, James, who could sleep through the worst thunder storms.
Nothing scared him.

'TIS TIME

It has taken a while

To rouse the interest

Work on the focus

Find where we are,

Who we are

And gain acceptance.

We know who we are

And our value to society,

The enormity of our contribution.

But we have been unacknowledged,

Ignored and unappreciated.

We are the loggers, the producers.

We've lost many men, many communities

And many battles.

The enemy came from far and near

To hug the trees,

Thoughtlessly and mostly in ignorance.

Yes, it has taken a while

But there is hope

When our Premier said

Its time to hug a logger,

All of us.

And he said it more than once………

Before he became the Premier of British Columbia and Leader of the Provincial Liberal Party, Gordon Campbell served as Mayor of Vancouver. As Mayors we were both appointed to a Financial Advisory Committee by the Provincial Government. He was the big city Mayor and I represented a coastal forestry-dependent Town. I realized that he had little awareness of the forest Industry and knew very little about the Truck Loggers Association (TLA), the most important industry association in the province. I invited him to attend the TLA Annual Convention with me when he became Leader of the Liberal Party and Leader of the Official Opposition in the Provincial Parliament. He attended and was given a V.I.P. welcome by then TLA President Ken Dyson. He has attended every single TLA Convention since. I wrote this poem after one of his major convention addresses to the TLA.

TO A HAGGIS

The people of the Scottish Race,

Around the world have left their trace,

With sports as wild as Toss the Caber

And Curling games for us to savour.

Their men dress up in funny skirts

Wild tartans decorate their shirts.

Their music comes from bags and pipes,

The cause of much complaints and gripes.

And then they boast about their food

And tell us that it's really good.

A friend of mine from down in Norwich,

Got really sick from Scottish porridge.

And when they honour the birth of Burns

They cook a dish, one's stomach turns.

They take the guts from very deep

Within the belly of some sheep.

They mince them up and add some spice

In hopes that you will think it's nice.

They play the pipes whose awful bleating

Will take your mind off what you're eating.

It's Scotland's way to really nag us,

With the secret weapon they call Haggis.

TO A HERON

Lone sentinel of the breaking day

In the orange glow of sunrise, grey,

Standing at and with attention, still,

Waiting patiently, impassively, I wonder will

The tide's edge glimmering at your feet

Cast up the food such patient strength must eat.

The crows around appear to find their fill,

The seagulls too, all seem to eat at will,

You stand disdainful yet, look down and then away,

Alert, Aloof, Alone, Selective, a Gourmet.

The sight of a patient heron standing at the tide's edge for hours shows grim determination and a willingness to work for what they get. These two poems were written for a "morning" heron and for an "evening" heron. There's a message there.

TO A HERON, AGAIN!

What's this, that does so smoothly glide

From out the mist, to land at ocean's side,

In fading light as daylight slips away

The Heron floats on wings of grey,

With legs outstretched at water's edge it lands

Until a tasty bite swims by, it patiently just stands,

Then lightening fast the long neck bends

The life of a small fish so quickly ends,

To keep life in that graceful bird

It's nature's way, it's even nature's word.

But once it has some food to eat, it spreads its wings to fly

Along the shore to another spot, beneath the same grey sky.

Once more it lands upon the shore and folds each gracious wing,

It's sad that such a lovely bird can look so good, yet cannot sing.

TO A KIPPER

In the British Isles there are many styles,

Of breakfast meals to please us,

That suit the taste of the human race,

In a way that's most ingenious.

Continental fare is always there,

With toast and buns so nice,

With milk and tea and black coffee,

Your appetite to spice.

There's big meals too, that will please you,

And put strength in your legs,

With sausage meat, that's a tasty treat,

And different kinds of eggs.

But there's a dish, a kind of fish,

The choice of those much hipper,

With more bones than meat, it's hard to eat,

It is the lowly kipper.

And there are those, and why God knows,

Who love this bony dish,

Who skip the rest and think it's best,

To breakfast on a fish.

TO A WINNER

The poet, Rudyard Kipling,

When just a young stripling,

Wrote many an inspiring poem,

Though in his young life

He dealt with the strife

Of a cold and detached foster-home.

His masterpiece "If"

Was a little bit stiff

And encouraged each man to be strong,

To muster his wit,

To succeed, never quit,

Be true and you'll never go wrong.

He implies that winning

Is closer to sinning

Unless you can do it with grace,

So greet your opponent

In the heat of the moment,

With a handshake and smile on your face.

Please keep in your mind,

It pays to be kind

Good sportsmanship always shines through.

The challenge is clear,

Be strong, do not veer,

The loser next time could be you.

The poem "If" by Rudyard Kipling is one of my favourite poems. Kipling was born in India and his very British parents sent him to a foster home in England when he was about seven years of age. He was brought up to keep a "stiff upper lip", be fair, be kind and know how to handle your wins and your losses with a sense of humour. This poem is dedicated to my grandchildren and their pals who have acquired these traits.

TO A WOMAN WHO NEVER SAID, "IF ONLY."

A EULOGY

As the oldest son in our family, it was my duty to provide some remarks on my mother's passing.

I have included them in my poetry book as a tribute to a great lady who maintained a positive and optimistic attitude throughout her life.

TO A WOMAN WHO NEVER SAID, "IF ONLY"

In the passing of our mother, Lily Furney, there is no sadness, just celebration. There is a joy that she lived for 91 years, generally healthy, always happy, upbeat and thoughtful. She was a reliable friend. She was strong willed, tough when necessary and didn't take "no" for an answer. She was confident in a happy marriage, which overcame the then prevalent bigotry and misunderstanding when young people from different religious backgrounds met and fell in love in the Ireland of the nineteen twenties.

Her love for Jim Furney never waned, even during his years in Australia, and it strengthened and blossomed from their marriage day to Jim's death in 1987.

She happily accompanied him on his many fishing trips to British Columbia, and accepted with loving resignation, his parting words when he headed off for a day's fishing, "expect me when you see me". She was a wonderful wife, and a wonderful mother.

When James and I were one and a half and three years of age, she was blessed with a daughter, Elizabeth, who was the joy of the household for the next three years. When Elizabeth died at that early age, we never heard my mother complain or bemoan the loss of her baby daughter. She accepted God's will. She got on with life, and we never ever heard her say "if only".

Brought up in Cork by a doting father and mother, with sister Violet and brother Willie and John, (all of whom predeceased her), she enjoyed the city life for most of her younger years. In 1957 on the death of her father, Gerald Fitzgerald, she and Jim took over his farm in Glanworth and she became a hard-working farmer's wife. The farm had been leased out for many years and needed a huge investment of time and money to make it viable. But with her sleeves rolled up, she took on the responsibilities and learnt about farming the practical way. Many great meals were produced in the refurbished farmhouse, to farm workers, contractors, relatives and friends. Her hospitality was legendary. Active and productive farming continued until Jim passed away in 1987 after his last fishing trip to British Columbia.

For most of the past ten years, she watched with joy, over the growing flock of grandchildren and great grandchildren. All of us, family and friends alike, benefited from her strongly-held moral principles, and her adherence to her even stronger Christian principles. She accepted gratefully the love and kindness of her family, her friends and especially her daughters-in-law.

She was everything a mother and wife should be. She never hesitated to stand up for her beliefs, her family, her friends and her neighbours, and she never gossiped.

She lived and practiced the golden rule, and she never said, "if only'.

May she rest in peace.

TO CARMEL

I wish I had the gift to write,
A poem of love with all my might.
But that for me is rather hard,
I lay no claim to being a bard.
However, to continue on,
I'll try to write some lines upon,
The things I like in you the best,
It's time I got them off my chest.
I met you when you were a child,
Your innocence had me beguiled.
To me you were a sweet young thing,
One look from you made my heart sing.
You were so lovely, sweet and pure,
My love for you would long endure.

I knew right then that this was it,
Into my life you had to fit.
From that time on, I tried to make
You love me just for my own sake.
To you alone I remained true,
And stayed away from girl-friends new.
My happiness you made complete,
My life had never been so sweet.
I love your looks, your walk, your smile,
In every way you are my style.
Your eyes are bright; your lips are true,
Above all else, you love me too.
And so I'm really glad to say,
Our love gets stronger day by day.

TO CLANCY....

The night has fled, another day is here
The birds are chirping in the trees their voices sweet and clear,
The town awakes, and leaves behind the dark
And from your kennel comes your morning bark.
At first it's gentle, then it turns to gruff
You're telling all the world you've had enough
It echoes from your kennel clear and deep
For kids and mom and dad, there's no more sleep.
Your head appears from out your kennel door
You look around and then you bark once more
You stretch your legs and arch your muscled back
Reluctant to step from your cozy shack.
You amble out to answer nature's call
And choose a spot along the neighbour's wall.
You sniff the trees and make your morning rounds
Ensuring that no visitor has crossed across your bounds.
Another bark, a scratch, against the big front door
To let us know you've guarded us throughout the night once more,
You bark and growl and scratch again, creating quite a din,
Reminding James and Liza that it's time to let you in.
You check the hall, the dining room, then flop upon the mat,
It's plain to see from your lazy sighs you've had enough of that.
You rest your head upon your paws you're thinking very deep
That after all this exercise you need to catch some sleep.

Written to prove that I could actually write a poem.

My son, when he was about ten years of age, was impressed with my first poem on a Heron, but did not believe that I wrote it. I told him that I was inspired by what I saw from our living-room window the previous morning. He challenged me to write a poem on what I saw looking out our kitchen window on the following morning. I looked out and saw our dog coming out of his kennel and stretching himself, then going through his usual routine. I left the poem, hand written on the breakfast table before I headed off to work. When I got home from work that night, both my kids said, "touché"!! The next "Clancy" poem was written after we had to have him put down after fifteen years as a very important part of our family.

CLANCY

TO CLANCY, NO ORDINARY DOG

You were just a pup, when the kids said, "Dad,
If you want to make, your two kids glad,
You will come with us to the house next door
Where they have some puppies that you'll adore".
Well we went to look, and we saw you there
You were pretty small, but had lots of hair,
We brought you home, with happy sighs
While our Mom looked shocked and feigned surprise.

She questioned my judgment, made quite a fuss,
But within two minutes, you were one of us.
You captured our hearts, with your lazy ways
As you slept your way, through those happy days,
We all thought that you were kinda neat
And love for a pup is a two-way street.
The kids looked after your hunger and thirst
And at suppertime they fed you first.

You would then come in, and watch us eat
As you lay content, at someone's feet.
A family dog, you soon became
And all you lacked, was a suitable name.
There was nary a name, that caught our fancy
'Till, the kids suggested, the name of "Clancy".
Now there was a name, with a stately ring
Fit for the dog, of a queen or king.

You carried the name, with a regal air
'Though your Dad was only, a small-town Mayor.
That name was famous, along the street
There wasn't a neighbour, you didn't meet
It would be hard, to try and pick
A neighbour you didn't, sniff or lick.
The dogcatcher who, hunts dogs with glee
Never tried to catch, old dog "three three".

Continued………

Continued……..

Another dog, to the pound he'd cart
But you had captured, even that man's heart.
You loved to go on camping trips, and learnt to live in tents,
And scared away wild animals, by spreading nasty scents.
You often went to places, that were really so remote
That the only way to get there, was to travel there by boat
Sea-legs you developed, when you were just a pup
And never on a sea-trip, did you ever once throw up.

The family sure enjoyed the time, that we all spent with you
And struggled with the question, as to what we'd ever do
If we should ever lose you, for whatever reason
Especially if it happened, before the Christmas Season.
We noticed in the last few months, that you were slowing down
Especially when we took you, for a walk around the town.
The time we took to do the walk, just took a little longer
Than in our early walking days, when we were both much younger.

Age was catching up with you, and slowing down your heart
And we had to prepare ourselves, for when you would depart.
It was hard on everyone of us, to see you look so sick
And it was even harder, when we saw you fade so quick.
The kids and Mom were with you, as you went upon your way,
And fifteen years of happiness, came to an end that day.
The parting wasn't easy, the hurt won't easily end
As all of us have lost, a most beloved friend.

A Eulogy to our family's best friend.

TO ELIZABETH

Two little boys, six and four and a half.
A sweet little daughter of three.
A proud mother and a happy father
Who didn't say much, but whose pride showed
In the way he worked and provided for his family,
In a small terrace house on the rim of the bowl that is Cork City,
In the mid-nineteen thirties.
One day, a visit by a gray-haired man, with a black leather bag,
And tubes hanging out of his ears, checking my three year old sister.
Mother and doctor talking quietly in sombre tones.
Mother acting normal, trying to hide her concern about a serious disease.
Neighbors sitting up all night, taking shifts, tending the very sick baby.
Suddenly, no more visits from doctor, no more neighbours taking shifts,
Something strange had happened.
Life and household almost back to normal for the two little boys.
It was Christmas Week.
My father and his best friend borrowed a car, parked it near our front door.
My mother told us two boys to go to the front room and stay quiet.
We heard muffled voices, footsteps coming down stairs.
More muffled voices, front door closing.
I remember peeking through the curtains
And seeing my father and his friend
Carrying a white box, carefully, down our front steps,
Putting it in the back seat of the car, and driving away.
My mother called us into the kitchen
And told us to get ready for a trip to Town,
To buy some Christmas presents.
Like the stoic she was,
She never said what was in the white box.

My mother had a backbone of steel. She was a Catholic who married a Protestant who had been disowned by his family. She never met her in-laws. She never complained or even mentioned the in-laws. Instead, she created a happy household in which my dad, who became a Catholic, was the head of a happy family with two sons and a daughter. My sister got very sick at the age of three and died just before Christmas in 1939. Both my parents were stoics as they accepted the loss of their only daughter and made arrangements quietly for a coffin and a burial. My brother, at four was too young to be aware of what happened, but I, as a six year old understood what was happening. What I could never understand was that I never saw my mother or father shed a tear and my mother took us shopping for Christmas presents on the day the body was taken to be buried This poem is written from my memories of that day.

TO FLOURISH

A fact that each person around us should know,

Is that it's from acorns that big oak trees grow.

Now, if acorns fall on good fertile ground,

It will not take long for there to be found,

Some offspring that came from a nearby oak tree,

As healthy young shoots growing up strong and free,

But if by a chance they're bent for some reason,

By twisting strong winds or snow in its season,

They will not grow up so tall, or so straight,

As trees they'll turn out, to be second rate.

Now there is a moral to this little story,

Just think of trees growing, in all of their glory.

A child like a tree, is so much the same

It needs from its folks much more than a name.

It should have surroundings without stress or strife,

In those so important first years of its life.

Where a tree needs good ground to help it grow strong,

A child needs a family where it can belong,

To develop good skills and learn how to nourish

The strength that it takes to survive and to flourish.

This is a reminder to all parents and teachers on how vulnerable our children are to bad example, especially in their formative years. Please read and heed.

TO MARK

I'm kinda lonely driving home,
So I will try to write a poem
Just like my ol' pal Gerry does.
Without being spotted by the fuzz.
I've got a sheet of paper here
Upon the seat beside me, near,
I've also got a pen or two,
But do not have the slightest clue,
What I should write a poem about
As I am heading to the south.
I know that I have lots of time
To come up with a fancy rhyme.
But as the milestones hurtle by
It matters not how hard I try,
To figure just where I should start,
The thinking almost breaks my heart.
I worry 'bout each passing truck
And almost hit a five point buck.
Then nearly lost my pilot's poise,
My God, that rumble strip makes noise.
At last I reach the Silver Bridge,
Five minutes to my beer-filled fridge,
Where I will crack a beer or two
To drown my sorrows, wouldn't you?

To honour a great family friend, Mark Murphy. He spent all his school holidays with our family in Port McNeill and was always reluctant to head back to Campbell River and school. After one of these holidays I arranged a flight back to Campbell River for him with a friend of mine, Bob Early, in a Trans Mountain Air float plane. Bob let Mark try out the controls and by the time they got to Campbell River, Mark had decided to become a bush pilot. He has been flying every since, a great pilot. He visits us regularly and in bad weather will drive up in his pickup truck. I told him that I wrote many poems during the 240 mile drive to and from Campbell River. He tried and gave up, so I wrote this in his honour. Mark's dad Dr. Richard Murphy, served Campbell River for many years. He was from Kinsale, County Cork, Ireland. (see Driving, Thinking, Writing)

TO SAM HIGGINSON

One night as I was working late, many years ago,
I answered a call from someone, whom I didn't know.
"I need oil pails delivered, and don't say no
It's leaking out fast, from under Milligan's hoe.
Head to Hyde Creek now, don't take anymore calls,
You'll find me in the mud, in my coveralls."
"But who are you", says I, "for you seem to know who I am",
"Don't worry boy, I know you, and you'll soon know me as Sam".
I called Danielle to report, that I'd be home by eight.
I didn't expect Sam's conversation, to go on all that late.
We topped up the oil, and he called it a day,
Sam knew I'd missed dinner and insisted I stay.
We became friends that night, as we shot the breeze,
The 40 years between us, we dispatched with ease.
Age was not an issue, for we saw eye to eye,
I soon figured out, I'd see much more of this guy.
"Now have one of Louise's beers, you should quench your thirst
And then we'll play some pool, and I break first".
Two bits for a game, became 4, then 6, then 8,
My financial losses only ended, when it got very late.
I came back home broke, from my first Sam meeting,
But the fun I had that night, ensured a repeating.
When I got home past midnight, Danielle gave me a look,
I explained what I learned that night wasn't written in a book.
I was thrilled to have a new friend, now he's been one for years.
He's hustled 200 of my dollars, but I've drank 300 of his beers.
We hit it off right from the start and right until the end,
I can tell you with great pride, that I call Sam my friend.
The future will be a bit strange, without our good friend here
Now as he looks down upon us try not to shed a tear.
Instead let's celebrate, the great chance we've had to know him
And so to all whose lives he's enriched, I dedicate this poem.

Presented in the eulogy for Sam Higginson
By James Furney, June 2007
This poem was written by my son James as part of the eulogy for our friend Sam Higginson.
Sam's widow, Louise, was the daughter of Whitey and Olive Souch who are mentioned in
poems about Whitey, elsewhere in this book. It is included in this collection in honour of
Sam and in respect of the poetic talents of James.

TO THE DUKE

In the mid nineteen sixties when times were the best,

Young people were told to succeed you go West.

So folk from the Prairies, Alberta, Man., Sask.,

Who liked to work hard, would try any task,

Came out to B.C. and its rugged West Coast,

To see if indeed there was truth to the boast,

That in B.C. as they'd often been told

The streets were all paved with silver and gold,

Where everyone had a fair choice or a chance,

Creating a fortune or losing their pants.

Now one of that group had a very strong hunch

That hard work would put him ahead of the bunch.

He had served his time as a butcher of meat

So butchering wood would be ever so neat.

He signed as a logger to a wild West Coast show,

His spirits were high, his finances were low.

Trees he could fell and logs he could buck,

He learnt to skin cat and drive logging truck,

He learnt to blast rock and to build a good road.

And how to get maximum logs on a load,

His bosses were happy, the outfit did well

'Twas time to retire and the outfit they'd sell.

Continued.........

Continued………

So banks were called in to finance the deal,

An offer accepted and ready to seal.

With all of his savings he signed on the line,

Convincing his family that all would be fine.

The planning was simple, straightforward the aim,

We'll make this here outfit the best in the game.

We'll take every chance that we can to expand.

The gamble paid off, just the way that they planned.

They hired the best loggers, the smart thing to do,

Each proud to be part of a real hi-ball crew.

They're led by a man they consider a prince,

Who barks out his orders so loud that they wince.

But no one complains, and they never rebuke,

This leader of men whom we know as the Duke.

This poem is about a young prairie lad from Saskatchewan who came west to try his hand at logging. He started out in an isolated logging camp on the North West coast of Vancouver Island. He soon learnt the ropes and worked hard for many years until he was offered the opportunity to buy the company he was working for. His two sons co-manage the company today and are settled with their families in Port McNeill. They are big supporters of our community and are in the forefront of many community projects.
Dedicated to David and Linda Dutcyvich and their two great sons, Chris and Eric.

TO THE SILLY FILLY IN THE FRILLY TILLEY

There's a legion of interesting people out there,

Who dress in a way that is most debonair.

They're seen in so many far out tourist places

With happy and cheerful big smiles on their faces.

They look like they've dressed for life in the wild,

But seem to prefer a routine that is mild.

Their clothing is rugged, 'twould take lots of wear,

It's elegant, tasteful, well-chosen with care.

The look of the clothing is khaki-like cream,

It oozes high-class in a way that's supreme.

The range of their clothing from trousers to shirts,

Includes belts and jackets and fine ladies' skirts.

Now all of these items are crowned by a Tilley,

Which makes some hat-wearers look really quite silly.

Its fame is oft' told in a legend quite gory,

So hard to believe, such a crazy hat story.

It seems that an elephant, quite on the sly,

Was watching a tourist who was standing nigh,

When all of a sudden the beast moved its trunk

And his hat joined the rest of its lunchtime food junk.

Continued………

Continued………

The story is told that some zoo-hand did stoop

To gather and check out this elephant's poop.

They found that the hat had completed its trip

With nary a mark from the elephant's grip.

So if you should go to where elephants thrive,

And one of the beasts starts to eat you alive.

Your one-of-a-kind Tilley hat with your name

Will ensure that you will not have died there in vain.

The hat will come through, but there will be no trace

Of yourself, just a satisfied smile on its face.

So you should make sure that you clearly inscribe

Your name on your hat as it's sure to survive.

The famous Tilley Hat is so Canadian that I felt it deserves a special poem. Wearing one on one's travels is an immediate declaration that you're Canadian, almost better than wearing a Maple Leaf.

TO WALT & EILEEN MCCONVILLE

Oh, Walt, Oh, Walt, please put a halt,

To each new clever poem.

They drive me very very close,

To leaving home sweet home.

My brain is drained, my mind is strained

By each poem from your den.

So, I concede and now I plead,

Eileen, remove his pen.

And now I s'pose, I should join those

Who send their Christmas wishes.

Just take the time, you're in your prime,

Help Eileen with the dishes.

And while it's clear, we're very near,

To Anno D. '06,

I hope, old son, you'll have more fun,

And still get in your licks.

I first came in contact with Walt when he sent us some entries in a Limerick contest that I organized to publicize the lack of roads and ferries in and to Northern Vancouver Island in the early nineteen sixties. We have communicated in poetic notes for many years and this poem was my reply to a clever Christmas greeting poem for Christmas in 2006.

TODAY'S THE DAY!

A certain thought occurs to me

That yesterday is history.

Tomorrow we can plainly see

Is still an unknown mystery.

And that just leaves us with today.

So please hear what I've got to say,

As I with certainty announce,

This is the only day that counts.

Too bad if this illusion shatters,

Today's the only day that matters.

A dozer boat in the "booming grounds", where logs were sorted by species.
(Fir, Spruce, Hemlock (Alaska Pine), Balsam, Cedar)

TUGBOATS/TOW BOATS

The foghorn warns that fog is rolling in,

The skipper sees that light is growing dim.

With seas aheaving, waves are growing large,

The deckhand looks astern and eyes the barge

Which rises high on each succeeding wave,

While diesel engines every effort gave

To stay ahead of such a heavy tow,

Full speed ahead, there's nowhere else to go,

While tug and barge are tossed around like toys,

This surely separates the men from boys.

In calmer weather, tug and barge are seen

To sail along so regal and serene,

Enhancing each and every seascape view,

The shore-bound, jealous of that tugboat crew.

But when the weather turns and seas get rough,

To keep your balance on the deck is tough.

Waves roll o'er the deck and through the scuppers,

The cook can't even make the crew their suppers.

At times like that the toughest job of all

Is making sure the engines do not stall.

The engineer and oiler down below,

Work 'round the clock, are always on the go,

While normally the engines roar away,

The crew takes them for granted day by day.

Each man on board's a member of the team,

In work conditions best described "extreme".

Continued………

Continued……..

With all shipshape from bow right through to rudder,

A ship at sea is just like any other,

But tugboats surely are a breed apart,

The reason that they steal each crewman's heart,

Their every moment ruled by that towline.

The skipper must take care, somehow define

The influence of each and every tow,

How much towline, the safest speed to go.

This trade cannot be learnt at any schools,

Except to learn the navigating rules.

There's no short cut to really learn the trade

And all the tough decisions to be made.

The skill required to keep them off the rocks

Comes at the tugboat College of Hard Knocks.

This poem is written as a special toast

To all the tugboat crews along the Coast.

Tugboats are a familiar sight up and down the British Columbia coast. They, with their barges, are the work horses that carry the majority of goods that are needed to keep the isolated coastal communities functioning. They haul logs to the sawmills, woodchips and chemicals to the pulp mills, gravel and cement to construction projects, petroleum products for industry and freight trucks back and forth between Vancouver Island and the Mainland. They will haul anything, anywhere. Harry Mose, a past Mayor of Port Hardy and Pete Tobey, a retired tugboat skipper have both told me some hair-raising stories dealing with tugs, tows, tides, winds and currents. This poem is dedicated to the two of them and all who sail in tugboats.

For my Daughter, Elizabeth

VALEDICTORIAN, THE FIRST STEP

Reluctantly, I faced a three hundred mile drive
On a Sunday afternoon, trying to put off
The moment of departure,
Your mother flatly refused to come with us,
With the excuse that your brother would be "home alone".
It was up to your Dad to do the deed.
You were to start school on Monday morning
In a Boarding School in Victoria,
For all the right reasons,
Even though it felt wrong.
The packing took a long time
And we dawdled in loading the car.
Finally a tearful departure
Your young brother holding his, bravely.
Your mother breaking down in floods,
Me, biting my lip, feigning bravery,
A mournful look on Clancy Dog's face.
Three hundred interminable miles of stilted conversation,
Neither of us wanting to discuss why.
Navigating the maze of streets to the School.
The formalities of signing you over to strangers
Who would guide you through grade twelve
And give you the incentives and inspiration,
Which would offset the negativism
Of some of the square pegs in round holes
Teaching at your grade eleven school.
Would this be better?
We didn't know, but the decision was made.
Grit your teeth, bite your lip again,
Be brave and hope for the best.
Unload your things, check out your dorm,

Continued........

192

Continued………

Say hello to the polyglot group

Of Mexican, Japanese, Chinese and other internationals,

Size up the kindly matron

Whose first question was, "did she bring a mug?"

The answer was "No".

Jump in the car, drive in all directions,

Found an open-late Sunday-night Drugstore

Yes, they had mugs, masculine, work-men's mugs,

Bought a Japanese-made look-alike antique one,

Which advertised "Shooting Irons & Sporting Accessories",

Brought it back to the Dorm, which by now,

In that darkening September evening,

Was beginning to look like a hut

In a Concentration Camp.

Doubts flooded my mind, was this the right thing to do?

Leaving you amongst strangers,

Strange classmates, strange teachers

And strange circumstances?

A heart-wrenching final goodbye,

You standing alone and vulnerable in the dusk

On the mound near the entrance gate.

Me, driving away, trying to hold back the tears,

Unsuccessfully, and facing another three hundred

Of the toughest miles I ever drove………

The quality of a school system is dependent on good teachers who want to teach for the right reasons. When a group of Secondary School teachers start to spend more time on their "retirement" planning than on teaching, a rot sets in and the students suffer. We saw this happen and worried about the stultified atmosphere created by a few tired school teachers who were counting the days to their retirement and who were preventing "new blood" from entering the system. It was time to find a better alternative for our daughter who was entering grade twelve. The alternative was St. Margaret's Boarding School in Saanich, where she had a great year and was their Valedictorian on graduating. As this prose verse about it indicates, it was the toughest and most difficult decision our family had ever made.

VANCOUVER ISLAND SECRET

The people in the Island South have lacked.

Appreciation of a simple fact,

There is a land beyond the Malahat.

Regardless of what they may think of that.

If questioned they just might admit they know,

A town that they have heard of, Nanaimo.

There's some among them who may be aware

Of Courtenay, Campbell River, way up there.

Their ignorance just makes me want to laugh.

They know so little 'bout the other half.

This Island stretches north three hundred miles,

Surrounded by a myriad smaller isles.

Majestic peaks reach upward to the sky,

A trillion trees across its valleys lie.

With snow-capped mountains storing winter snows,

The source of all those stream and river flows.

A thousand lakes bejewel this lovely land,

As nice a place as Nature ever planned.

One of the greatest places on this earth,

Its harbours offer all a pleasant berth.

Its seas alive with every kind of fish

A place to fulfill every sportsman's wish.

With forests ever green and mountains grand,

It is the best kept secret in the land.

VENGEFUL PATÉ

A logging camp life was not great,
For me and Tom Murphy my mate.
On weekends we had some time off,
Each logger dressed up like a toff.
We took a speed-boat to the Bay,
Our demons intending to slay.
The old Nimpkish Inn was the spot
And beer we consumed there a lot.
By midnight no one could feel pain,
Head down to the speed-boat again.
We'd built up a big appetite,
While drinking that beer through the night.
The pub did not serve any food
As eating while drinking was rude.
And as we staggered down the ramp,
We hoped we'd find some food in Camp.
The speed-boat dropped us at the dock,
The time was almost one o'clock.
Lights were on in the rigger's shack
Food to cure our hunger attack?
We each were packing lots of beer,
Two cases each of liquid cheer.
We hoped that he'd be in the mood,
To share our beer and offer food.
The rigger greeted us in style,
Upon his face a thirsty smile.
He took a good look at our beer
And said, "by God, your welcome here."
His wife stood there a 'yawning deep.
'Twas obvious she needed sleep.
"Sandwiches for these hungry boys,
We'll drink some beer, one of life's joys."

Continued........

Continued……..

His wife was cross, she shook her head,

She was about to go to bed.

The rigger sat and cracked a beer

And handed her the bubbly cheer.

So to the kitchen off she went

No more objections, seemed content.

A tray of sandwiches in style,

Presented with a vengeful smile.

We finished off the tasty food,

Sharing tales with the rigger dude.

But then as we got up to go,

I felt the need to really know,

What was the name of the paté,

Which we had eaten off that tray.

Into the kitchen, take a look,

What type of paté did she cook?

There on the counter clear in sight,

Two empty cans of cat food, light.

And as we staggered on our way

I heard her call and clearly say,

"I hope you liked that great paté."

*"Written in honour of a logger's wife who got fed up with her husband because of his
Saturday night drinking parties. For variety, she would sometimes substitute canned dog
food instead of cat food, when she got the job of feeding her husband's beer drinking pals."*

VERY CHEEKY

There are some guys who think its best

To contemplate a female breast.

But I think that these guys are dumb,

I much prefer a female bum.

So on this day just to be kind,

She put tight jeans on her behind.

She knew that this would cause a fuss,

Amongst the guys aboard the bus.

And as we watched those jean seams strain,

We suffered from such pleasant pain.

With thoughts of pleasure we could seek,

If we could take a little peek.

At what was wrapped inside those jeans,

We knew we'd stoop to any means.

And as we thought of each tight cheek,

We knew that we were all too weak.

To suavely say with polished ease,

Please let us give your orbs a squeeze.

We know it would be good for you,

And give us lots of pleasure too.

The thought is sweet, a bit extreme,

A little cheeky, but we dream.

VICHYSSOISE

Our land is like cold vichyssoise

With Capital in Ottawa.

And like that soup our country's cold,

If it's not stirred, it starts to mould.

It also claims to be half French,

A claim that some would rather quench.

As with the soup, it does occur,

This country is quite hard to stir.

Strong feelings 'neath the surface lurk,

But 'twill take passion and hard work.

Complacency's a sad disease,

Which could be changed with patient ease.

And yes, it would be rather neat

To just supply a little heat.

There maybe something we can do,

To turn this cold soup into stew.

Hard work is better than to rue,

I guess it's up to me and you.

This poem was written to encourage people to understand and appreciate what a fabulous country we live in. We are all so lucky to live here

WHAT ARE THE CHANCES?

It looks like pre-ordination to me!

Otherwise,

Why would I get up from a warm

New Year's Eve fireplace

And at the nagging, or behest,

Of my mother,

I headed down-town in Cork City,

Knowing that all the tickets

For all the New Year's Eve dances,

Would have been sold weeks earlier.

Cork was a dancing town in 1959.....

A predictable shake of the head

From the doorman at the Imperial Hotel.

"No, buddy, not a chance,

Not a ticket left, anywhere."

I walk away and stroll down Pembroke St.,

Past Canty's Pub.

Jeeze, isn't that where the Band

Has a drink before they go to work!

Walk in; know most of the Band,

"Hey, Ger, how's things in Canada?

Good to see you again."

"Well, lads, things are great in Canada,

But not so good in Cork.

Continued.........

Continued.........

I can't get into the Imperial,

Tickets are all sold."

"Bobby, give Gerry the trombone,

And he goes in with the Band,

Just like old times."

What are the chances?

I slide past the doorman

With the boys in the Band.

Don't know a soul there,

But recognise a few faces, however.

I've been away over six years,

There you were, tweed skirt,

Pale yellow sweater, straight back,

And grabbed by one of your many fans

For every bleedin'dance.

The Bishop of Cork had decreed,

No dancing on Sundays

And this was Saturday night.

When they called the last dance,

At ten minutes to twelve,

I was standing next to you

And had decided that this dance

Was the most important of my life.

You said "yes,"

And we danced into 1960.

And the rest of our lives,

Together.

Continued.........

Continued.........

I drove you home the long way,

And we dated 'til I left for Canada,

In April.

In the meantime you heard

All there was to know about sheep farming

And I met your family.

They seemed to like your shepherd.

And I managed to convince you,

That you might enjoy the adventure

Of working in an outpost hospital,

In Alert Bay, British Columbia

For a Doctor Jack Pickup.

You said, yes,

It was obvious that your Dad,

Had met my two plotting grandfathers,

Gerald Fitzgerald and Franks Furney, in Heaven,

And arranged the whole thing!

What are the chances?

Having lived in London, England for two years and in British Columbia for the next four years, I was out of touch with my generation when I returned to my hometown of Cork, Ireland for Christmas 1959. Because of heavy snow, logging and mining had shut down for the winter and my dad needed a hand with the farm, so I became a farmer for the next four months. Sitting at the fireside with my parents on New Year's Eve, I was content to spend the evening with them and catch up on all the news and family gossip that I had missed over the preceding six years. My mother told me to go to a dance and enjoy myself. After some protestations, I agreed and half-heartedly headed off. Little did I know what was in store for me and how it would change my life..........

The reference to my grandfathers is because I only knew my mother's father. I never knew my dad's father as he was a Protestant who disowned my father for marrying a Catholic. I'm convinced they have met in Heaven and have been working for me, ever since.

WHAT'S IN A NAME?

A rose by any other name,

Is still a rose, the very same.

Some things are not well taught in schools,

So think about these useful rules.

Be sure to keep them in your mind,

It will show, you are so refined.

Now in the army men are taught

To call their weapon what they ought.

With its name you do not trifle,

You must call your "gun" your rifle,

And should you ever go to sea,

Please take this good advice from me.

Try not to make a silly slip,

Be sure to call the "boat" your ship.

Dedicated to Marco Romero

When the first shipment of gravel was being shipped to California from the new Port McNeill Quarry, I was invited by the President of the company, Marco Romero, to join Chief Tony Hunt and Chief Bill Cranmer as guests aboard the Canadian Shipping Company ship the MV Acadian, under the command of Captain Filippov. We were accompanied by the Chairman of the Company, Harry Sutherland and Marco Romero, the President and CEO.

During the four day voyage, we had our meals at the Captain's Table and found Captain Filippov to be a most gracious host. During discussions, Marco Romero had a tendency to refer to the ship as "the boat". He was reminded regularly that it was a ship, (the rule being that you can put a boat on a ship, but you cannot put a ship on a boat).

I wrote a poem for Marco on the subject and the Third Officer prepared a copy which was formally presented at the Captain's Table.

WHINING

There is no doubt that in my time,
I've heard a lot of people whine,
Now in the North they will complain
About the weather and the rain.
Of course the further North you go,
Complaints will be about the snow.
And should you travel to the East,
The talk will be about the beast
Of Government in Ottawa,
And every bureaucratic law.
The people in the balmy South
Don't have a lot to bitch about.
They holiday where it is warm,
Winter golf, no snow the norm.
Which brings us to where snivelling's best,
'Way out here in the wild, wild West.
In this great portion of our land,
You'll find the whining really grand.
The bitching here would break your heart.
The whiners here all do their part.
Complaints about the Government,
Are voiced by every malcontent.
And it's the truth, these know-it-alls,
Just do not have the guts or balls
To take a chance, run for election.
May be fearful of rejection.
At least by running they could earn,
The right to speak on their concern.
So next time you hear someone whine
Just tell them not to waste your time.

Dedicated to those who like to complain but who do nothing but whine.

203

WHITEY'S NEW YEAR'S EVE PARTY

His name was Whitey,

We worked together

Keeping a mine-haul road open,

Ploughing snow with a grader,

Spreading sand

In one of our worst winters ever.

We each packed a six-cup thermos.

Liquid heat.

Sat in the cab of the grader,

For lunch and coffee breaks

When it got too cold.

Talked about the old days

As we sipped our coffee.

It helped us to forget

How cold we were.

Talked about the best

And the worst of times.

"Whitey", I said one day

"Tell me about the best,

Maybe it will warm us up."

Continued........

Continued.........

"Well", said Whitey,

"I was single at the time,

It was New Year's Eve

And we had a big dance

At the Community Hall.

The whole camp was there.

Wives, kids, the works.

After midnight I got kinda tired

And went up behind the stage

And fell asleep on a pile of curtains.

When I woke up,

I was alone and locked in.

They had all gone home,

But had forgotten to lock the booze cupboard.

The search party found me the next day,

At about three in the afternoon.

It was the best New Year's Eve I ever had."

These two poems about my good friend Whitey Souch, were written to honour a great workmate. Whitey had a slow and thoughtful way of expressing himself and these two poems will give you an insight on his style. He was a great guy to work with.

WHITEY'S UNDERSTATEMENT

The word "laconic" best describes

My old friend Whitey.

He took things in his stride,

Never panicked, never rushed, never complained,

Never slacked off at work.

You could rely on Whitey.

It was a sad day, when this part-time Gillnet-fisherman,

Pulled his Gillnetter onto the beach

At the mouth of Hyde Creek,

For the last time.

He and his lifelong partner Olive,

Settled into the old house on the property,

Where we and our kids visited regularly,

Christmas Day visits at mid-morning

Involved a warm welcome,

Hugs and handshakes,

And an exchange of presents,

Olive busily fussing,

Preparing goodies in the kitchen.

"Whitey" she says,

"Aren't you going to pour a drink for our visitors?"

"I guess so," says Whitey, as he heads for the rum and coke,

"And will you have a drink yourself?" asks Olive,

Whitey answered in his usual laconic tone,

With the understatement of the year.

"Probably".

WHO OWNS WHOM?

Our household once decided on a cat

To sit upon our welcoming door mat,

A cat that would not do what it was told,

It fitted in that "couldn't care less" mould.

Of cat egos we all have surely heard,

They preen themselves as much as any bird,

And should a bird come close within their grip,

That bird will just have made its final trip.

The scattered feathers soon will settle down,

The cat will quickly lose its hungry frown,

With tummy full of food and feeling good,

It's time to stroll around the neighbourhood.

It leaves the comfort of your cozy home

And you are left to worry all alone,

They'll spend the time in hunting, killing mice

And find the joy of mating rather nice.

When they are late returning you are worried

But cats when doing their duty won't be hurried.

It matters not how you may handle that,

The beast owns you, you do not own the cat!

WHO'S IN CHARGE?

Of Government levels there are four.
We should be thankful there's no more.
They run the Country, Province too,
Regional Districts, quite a few.
Then there is the one that's Local,
Best of all, tends to be vocal.

These local Councils seen as fair,
With Councillors led by a Mayor.
Hard working people serve on each,
Though sometimes seen as out of reach.
Prime Ministers, Premiers as well,
Live life in isolated hell.

Well fertilized, kept in the dark
Just like mushrooms, what a lark.
The voter thinks he's in control
When he goes to the voting poll.
He hopes his chosen one gets in,
But I have got bad news for him.

It matters not whom we elect
Or even whom we may reject,
Reality is simply that,
Things are run by the bureaucrat.
A simple fact, but rather large,
Bureaucracy's in total charge.

Those elected think it's their role
To exercise some slight control.
These politicians think it's them
But they should stop and think again.
They speak as if they really matter,
But sadly, that's just idle chatter.

WHO'S THINKING

It's sometime between midnight and daybreak.
It's cold and the rain is coming down in sheets.
The raindrops are bouncing on the tank tops.
And I am standing in my shelter on the catwalk
Thinking.

The oil barge is pumping gas and diesel.
At about the same volume as the rain falls,
All this fossil fuel to run the machines of industry,
Run people's cars, keeping them mobile and their houses warm.
I'm still thinking.

The geologists came up with the name, fossil fuels.
When they first dug for oil, they found some old bones.
They had no idea where the oil came from or who put it there,
So they assumed that it came from the animals,
I'm still thinking.

I'm thinking that with all the oil pumped daily,
From the supposed graves of all these animals,
There must have been one hell of a pile of dinosaurs
Piled as high as Mount Everest to fill all those oil wells.
I'm still thinking.

I think of the sheer volume of that oil,
Is it leaving an empty hole in the earth?
Can the ground surrounding that hole
Continue to support the earth's crust?
Now you can do the thinking!

World consumption of petroleum products is about eighty-six million barrels each day. I have always wondered about the name "fossil" fuels. Hence this verse written in the middle of the night on top of Shell's fuel tanks at Beach Camp, as they were being pumped full from a Seaspan oil barge. I also worry about the empty spaces left in the ground after oil wells are pumped dry. Do these vast empty spaces weaken the structure of the earth in any way? Do they cause earthquakes?

WIVES

As we sit 'round a yule-log fire,

Of pleasant thoughts we do not tire.

These thoughts inspired by friends like you,

Without such friends what would we do?

With pure goodwill our friendship thrives,

Encouraged by our loving wives.

Our blessings we can count aloud,

With wives of whom we are so proud.

We're pleased with all this Christmas Cheer,

And two companions we hold dear.

We're both two very lucky men,

Recorded by poetic pen.

This poem was written for my friends, Poet Walt McConville and his wife Eileen who have been producing magnificent poetry over the years. Walt entered our infamous limerick contest many years ago, when our community was trying to get the attention of Premier W.A.C. Bennett, so that he would allocate some provincial funding for roads and ferries to serve the Northern half of Vancouver Island.

YOU BETTS

Now and again some women and men
Will earn your admiration.
They pull their weight and live life straight,
They're the backbone of our Nation.
And of them all, I can't recall,
A one that better gets
My fondest praise for her honest ways,
Her name was Jenny Betts.
She lived her life, which had its strife
In the years of the Great Depression,
But she survived and somehow thrived
And made a great impression.

Now she was tough, no powder puff,
And didn't suffer fools,
She didn't shirk when she had to work
With axe and saw for tools.
I tell no lies, she cut railroad ties
With her dad and brothers too
'Til she met a man who was tall and tan,
Who fell for her Mulligan stew.
And so with pride, he moved his bride
To a place called Port McNeill,
Where he found a shack, with garden out back,
A war-time era deal.

Continued........

Continued......

Now she worked hard with her trusty pard,

Four kids arrived in time

Two girls, two boys were her little joys,

Four names I cannot rhyme.

She had a rule when they went to school,

They were never ever late,

So they did well, I'm proud to tell

And each did graduate.

Two teachers dear, an engineer,

Plus one in chemistry,

And to this day, they all display

Their strength as family.

Some time ago, she began to slow

Soon after Wallace died,

And there were tears in the past few years,

Without him by her side.

I could see a trend, in my old friend

When she made her final journey.

On one of those days, she gave me praise,

When she said "Good Mayoring, Furney".

She sipped her tea and smiled at me,

You can put away your pen,

I just know, it's time to go,

And I won't be back again.

This poem was written in respect for Wallace and Jenny Betts. They were among the first families to settle in the logging camp that became the Town of Port McNeill. Their volunteering efforts were a great example to others, who have followed in their footsteps. Our Town Council voted unanimously to make them Freemen of Port McNeill, the first couple to be so honoured. Our Town Council named Betts Boulevard for them.

YOU TWO HAVE

It's over twelve thousand midnights ago,

But seems so much less.

Your mother was getting tired

Of carrying you around in her tummy,

As she woke me from an all-too-short sleep

And said "it's time". It was midnight.

We dropped your two-year old sister

At Huggin's house with her pre-packed bag

And caught the waiting water-taxi at the dock.

After a bumpy, stormy ride across Broughton Strait,

We arrived at the hospital wharf in Alert Bay.

To our great relief, you had decided to stay where you were.

We walked to the hospital which was run

By an Administrator named Deadman

And a doctor named Pickup.

The Phillipino nurses gave me a coffee,

A gown and a mask.

The Doc said, "if you're going to faint,

Please fall backwards":

What! Me faint? Me, who had delivered

Twins and triplets on an Irish sheep farm!

But, I almost did faint, with joy,

As I held your mother's hand and said,

"It's a boy".

Continued………

Continued………

Two days later, the water-taxi ride home,

Into the arms of your first babysitter,

Your sister Liza.

There have been twelve thousand happy days

After all those midnights.

The first few words, the first few steps,

The bigger steps like kindergarten,

The Old School, Sunset School, North Island Secondary,

Brentwood College, graduating as Valedictorian.

The hockey, the softball, kayaking,

Camping and fly-fishing with your Grandad.

Your footloose year in Europe, the Iron Curtain,

The Berlin Wall and the peace of a farm in County Cork.

Then two U Vic. years, savouring Australia

As a Barkeep at Brisbane's Expo Irish Pub.

Circum-motoring that Continent,

Checking out South East Asia,

Before two more years and graduation from U. Vic.

As a commonsense environmentalist.

Not yet ready to settle down,

Weddings for your best friends,

Liza, Chris, Eric, Josh and Trev,

And others too numerous to mention.

A work routine, responsibility and

Middle of the night oil barges.

A relief girl called Danielle to work in the office

And who liked to shock.

Continued………

Continued………

Came to work one day, head shaved,

We were Mr. Cool, "Good morning, Danielle

Did you pick up the mail?"

Our long-term office stalwart, Les, returns to her job,

Danielle leaves for Central America

And my thoughts were, "that's too bad,

I kinda liked her short hair and her long temper,

Maybe she'll return and tell us about her trip".

She did, you listened, were duly impressed

And wanted to hear more.

Then you took her to Ireland.

She liked the Irish and their dancing.

You probably found each other in Lisdoonvarna.

You asked the question on the riverbank at your grandad's farm,

And her answer gave real meaning to the joined hands

Of your Claddagh friendship rings.

We should all be so happy and lucky enough,

To find someone

With whom we can hold hands for life.

You two have.

This prose-poem was written for, and read by me at the outdoor wedding of our son James and his wife Danielle. The wedding was held in front of their then unfinished home in Hyde Creek near Port McNeill, a pretty laid-back event to which everyone was invited. Surprisingly, no one fell in the pond.

YOU WON'T KNOW WHAT HIT YOU

What is love?

It is more than like.

It is the strongest form of like,

It goes far beyond like.

It is felt deep within us,

If we are lucky,

Lucky enough to experience it.

It is frustrating if unrequited,

It is frighteningly glorious if requited

It can be physical or mental

Or both.

It may be slow or sudden.

Can take months or years to develop and grow.

The first seed can be a glance

Or a glimpse

Or the touch of a hand in passing.

The clasp of a handshake.

It can be incidental or accidental.

Not forethought or fore-planned.

It can be all encompassing, all consuming,

Bitter or sweet.

It may be inspired by a smile,

The curve of a cheek,

The toss of a head,

It is illusive.

It is love.

"ON THE SQUARE"

At a Lodge meeting such as this,

It's great to feel fraternal bliss.

Where Brothers know that they belong

And with each other get along.

We're all from different walks of life,

All anxious to avoid the strife

That threatens us from day to day,

Freemasons have a better way.

Each Lodge has got a special tone,

Belonging to that Lodge alone.

Our strong traditions touch us all,

When answering the Master's call.

Our history has made us strong

Within the Lodge where we belong.

As Brothers we show how we care,

By always acting On the Square.

Live by our rules, the best you can,

So here's to you, Masonic man.

"A Toast"

*A friend of mine, Jim Jones, was at an evening meeting of his lodge. He used my poem
"Toast to the Ladies" page 15 to honour the ladies present.
He asked me would I write a similar poem to honour the men. Hence this poem to honour
his fellow members who always act honourably "On the Square".*

THE BLACK HAWK GANG RIDES AGAIN

A Garda Station, Saint Luke's Cross,

Where Sergeant Barry was the boss.

On the road called Ballyhooly,

Where the kids were most unruly.

The girls were really pretty good,

Around that tough-guy neighbourhood.

But when they had to deal with boys,

The Cork policemen lost their poise.

The Mayor and Council did their best

To handle the police request.

The Furney boys were bad, the worst,

So they're the ones we'll tackle first.

The very worst in all of Cork,

Much worse than gangsters in New York.

We'll send the toughest cop in Town,

To help to hunt the Furneys down.

This is a job for Duck-eye Finn,

Where others failed, Duck-eye will win.

So off he went to walk his beat

To make the Furney boys retreat.

But Duck-eye Finn had met his match,

The Furney boys he could not catch.

As they played foot-ball on the street,

All by the rules, they did not cheat.

Continued………

Continued.........

They played with hoops and tory tops

And managed to avoid the cops.

They always kept a sharp look-out,

Whenever Duck-eye was about.

He liked to creep from gate to gate,

Until one day, `twas getting late,

The kid on lookout fell asleep,

A'snoring and a'dreaming deep.

He did not hear old Duck-eye's feet,

Along the far side of the street.

And as we stood near Murphy's house,

Duck-eye walked up, quiet as a mouse.

"Aha," he said, "I've caught you all,

I'll summons you for playing ball,

Out on the street, against the law.

Give me your address, name your Paw".

I blurted out my street address,

I had no option, must confess.

I told him "Furney" was my name,

Street football was my special game.

He said, "You boys are very bad

I need each boy to name his Dad"

Our youngest pal whose name was Paddy,

Said, "my father's name is Daddy".

Then Duck-eye Finn began to laugh,

Continued.........

Continued………

So loudly it was off the graph.

He laughed so loud he could not stop,

A funny sight, a laughing cop.

The tears ran down his chubby cheeks

And left his face all marked with streaks.

To stop the tears he closed his eyes

And we began to realize,

We had a chance to run away

And live to play another day.

But that would not have been too fair,

`Cause Duck-eye caught us fair and square.

At last he stopped and wiped his eyes

And looked at us with great surprise.

"Real bad boys would have run away

There are no summonses today

And from now on, when you boys play,

Duck-eye will look the other way".

Growing up in Cork, Ireland during the nineteen forties there was very little vehicle traffic because of petrol rationing.
Us kids (we called ourselves the Black Hawk Gang) used the street as our playground for football, hurling, hoops, tops and other games.
It was against the law even though there was little traffic. The police patrolled on foot and tried to discourage us for safety reasons.
Avoiding the police became a game for us and added a bit of excitement to our lives. This poem is written in honour of one of these kindly policemen. He was a good sport.

"THE LAST SPOONFUL"

There's a Valley of Green Gold,

Hillsides with stands of the best timber

That Mother Nature can produce...

Snow-capped, rocky, craggy mountains

And a silver pure river running through it,

A breeding ground for salmon that nurtures them....

In time, it welcomes them back,

After their great ocean journey,

To start the whole process over again....

The trees are harvested carefully

And replanted two for one,

To ensure their healthy survival for the next harvest...

Communities of forest workers

Live in the Valley with their families,

Their labours contributing mightily

To the wealth of our province,

To the wealth of the shareholders

And the wealth of Governments at all levels,

Local, Regional, Provincial and Federal...

These people work hard for the security of their families,

For their happiness and their education...

Schools and recreation facilities flourish,

And everyone benefits...

Until the forces of environmentalism

Continued.........

Continued………

Come crashing down on the valley,

And many other valleys across our province.

Borne on the wings of questionable funding

Provided by wealthy, tax-free Foundations…

An inexplicable urge to please these forces,

Causes governments to increase regulations

And reduce the harvest levels…

The life-blood of the valley is choked off slowly.

People leave, facilities start to deteriorate

And the school lacks the number of students

That justifies its existence….

The high-school kids are the first to go,

Their faithful, long-term families,

Move away for the sake of their kids….

Soon, there are only six pupils

In the elementary school,

And it too is being closed…

The sound of their laughter at play,

No longer resounds in the Valley….

There are still some workers left,

But many drive in from other places,

Where schools and other necessary services exist…

But these people too, are threatened,

As the mighty forces of environmental do-goodism

Convince the Government

Continued………

Continued.........

That we no longer need to support or augment

Our resource-dependent economy...

It brings to mind the story of the man

Who figured that his dog could survive

With less and less food...

He reduced the dog's portion by a spoonful each day,

And was shocked when the dog died

On the day the last spoonful was eaten.

The hard reality is that our resource industries

Provide the food for all the people of these valleys,

For our whole province and for our whole country....

We are all being pushed closer and closer to the last spoonful...

The valley is now bereft of many of its people

And the only sounds left,

Are the gurgle of the sparkling river

And the whisper of the breeze,

As it stirs the lonely trees

In this great valley.

Small Coastal Resource Communities have been badly affected by a well-funded, mis-guided environmental movement that has plagued the forest industry, the mining industry and most recently, the aquaculture industry. This poem is written about an area that has been particularly affected and where the workforce is only a shadow of its former self.

THIS ONE'S FOR YOU!

By now you've had a chance to look

At the notes and poems within this book.

They cover subjects far and wide

And offer you another side

Of this man's take on West Coast life,

So peaceful in a world of strife.

These poems are only this poet's view,

With hopes that they will all please you.

These verbal pictures word by word

Describe some thoughts that have occurred

To me the painter of these pictures

Writ within poetic strictures.

My hope is that you have enjoyed

The many themes which I've employed,

But if to criticize you're prone

I guess you'll have to write your own.